Joy Skjegstad

STARTING A NONPROFIT AT YOUR CHURCH

Foreword by Mary Nelson

An Alban Institute Book
ROWMAN & LITTLEFIELD
Lanham • Boulder • New York • Toronto • Plymouth, UK

First Rowman & Littlefield paperback edition 2014

Published by Rowman & Littlefield
4501 Forbes Blvd, Suite 200, Lanham, MD 20706
www.rowman.com

10 Thornbury Road, Plymouth PL6 7PP, United Kingdom

Library of Congress Catalog Number 2002104641

ISBN 13: 978-1-56699-265-7 (pbk: alk. paper)

♾™ The paper used in this publication meets the minimum requirements of American National Standard for Information Sciences—Permanence of Paper for Printed Library Materials, ANSI/NISO Z39.48-1992.

Printed in the United States of America

*For Ethan Bradley Skjegstad Schrag,
whose birth spurred me on to a greater vision*

Contents

Foreword

Faith-based organizations are now in the limelight in this country. Government is explicitly including faith-based groups as eligible applicants for various funding efforts (subject to some constraints). Recent research on programs dealing with low-income, discouraged, drug-addicted, ex-offender, and other marginalized groups shows that a significant number of the most effective approaches and programs have a common faith basis. So the rush is on: Increasing numbers of churches are seeking to enter the fray, apply for government funding, tackle bigger problems, and capitalize on opportunities. In this moment of great possibility, Joy Skjegstad's how-to book is most timely and immensely useful.

The book is down-to-earth, written from an insider-practitioner's experience and through the perspective of faith. The style is easy to understand, with multiple concrete examples, checklists, and worksheets that should save congregational leaders from reinventing the wheel. It will shorten the work of committees and boards seeking to start a new ministry or enhance an existing one. I recommend this book to church and faith-based groups seeking to establish and operate programs in effective ways that enable them to keep focused on their purposes and mission.

In my experience, several important basics need to be kept in mind when dealing with faith-based community ministries. First, it is important to be clear about the faith perspective, the *reason* we are doing this ministry. It is just as important to be sure that the methods we use reflect those faith values and purpose.

Each person is made in the image of God and is loved by God. The gospel empowers and liberates people to seek justice in the land. So the methods we use must empower and liberate, building on people's capacities and the fullness of God's future. The gospel calls us beyond charity. The faith basis of our work should provide for a deeper understanding of the difference between offering handouts and transforming lives, between food pantries and job placement. All our time can be consumed in the immediate acts of charity unless we are intentional about the ultimate goal of transformation: enabling people to live the fullness of life as God intended. We must go "up the river" to discover the causes of the problems we are addressing and deal with them even while we pull drowning people out of the river. Faith-based action includes empowerment, advocacy, and standing with others in our efforts. Our charity efforts must not dull the edge of anger and energy to seek justice.

A second important aspect of faith-based community ministry has to do with the ongoing relationship between the initiative and the local church that gives birth to it. Often the initiative is begun with great idealism, but the mechanisms for carrying out the initiative and the relationship between the ministry and the church are not spelled out. The lack of clarity can soon lead to dissension and dilution of the effort. This book gives wonderful insight into the factors that should be addressed around this issue when setting up the initiative and suggests that the original decisions need not be permanent. It is important to think about the relationships early in the planning and to decide what structures and relationships will free up both the church and the organization to achieve ministry goals. But the relationship must be dynamic. Often successful ministry programs are simply spun off and thereby lose the vital connection to the faith basis and the church. Such decisions should be made with great care.

Leaders of faith-based initiatives also need to partner with others. The newest potential partner for churches is our government. The door is now open for more faith-based groups to apply for government funds. With that opportunity, however, comes the danger of blurring the lines between church and state. Government funds usually come with a lot of guidelines and restrictions. Without clear administrative expertise and separate accounting to ensure government funds are not mixed with church funds used to pay for religious activities, many a program and initiative will be in danger of allegations of misuse of government funds (even when misused innocently or unintentionally). Such situations will make it hard on other faith-based efforts to obtain government funds, which can be important resources. However, the most effective programs, those that seek long-term, sustainable results, have learned how to collaborate and partner with a whole host of institutions, including government, education, other churches and faith institutions, and businesses. Because the church cannot do it all by itself, collaborating and building on what each partner does well are essential.

The Jobs Partnership in Raleigh, North Carolina, is a good example of such collaboration. Working together are the business community (they provide employment and resources), a community college (government funds pay for skills trainers), and the community and supporting churches (they recruit the unemployed and provide participants Biblical training, mentoring, and companionship).

This moment of opportunity also presents a danger; the church does not do well when it is embraced by the culture and government. In these circumstances, we have too often lost our prophetic edge, blurred our vision and purpose, and chased after funds. So we stand in a creative tension as we move wholeheartedly into church-based community ministry

Finally, the special opportunity (which may not last long) that comes with heightened attention to faith-based community ministry means that we must "seize the day," move boldly. But when moving on this opportunity, we need to make sure that we are not sloppy, well-meaning do-gooders, but instead are good stewards of the opportunity and the resources. This means we must operate effective and efficient organizations that enable achievable and documented outcomes. To respond appropriately to God's call, we need to rely on books like this and sharing with each other what we are learning. Sustained by our "five loaves and two fishes," a lot of prayer and discernment, and God's staying power, we will be prepared to do justice and act with compassion in our communities.

MARY NELSON
President
Bethel New Life, Chicago

Preface

It's a Sunday morning in 1987 at Park Avenue United Methodist Church in South Minneapolis. The morning praise songs rise to a gospel crescendo, and the congregation is ready to hear a word about the weekday ministries of the church. The president of the Park Avenue Foundation rises to tell of all that has happened in the past week. His descriptions of the ministries are exciting; there is so much offered for young people and their families. Real needs are being met, and lives are being changed. Many of the partnerships and financial resources for the programs have come through the Park Avenue Foundation, a separate nonprofit established by the church.

I leave this service inspired and think to myself, "Running the Park Avenue Foundation would be the most exciting job in the world." Little did I know that I would have a firsthand experience with the job just a few years later when I was named executive director of the foundation in 1994, a position I held for five years. During those years I became convinced that church-based nonprofits can be the "engine" for new, exciting, and much-needed ministries all around the country.

While at Park Avenue, I connected with many other congregations attempting to implement the same nonprofit structure. People would come to me with incredible vision for ministry. "We want to provide housing for single mothers," they would say, or "God's given me a vision to help people who struggle with the same addictions that I have." There was no doubt in my mind that God had uniquely equipped these ministry leaders for the work.

What stood in the way, more often than not, was the management part. I have learned along the way that many congregations lack the technical knowledge and skills to set up a separate nonprofit. Many ministry leaders are unclear about legal requirements, board duties, fundraising, and establishing a clear vision, among many other management issues. Without these pieces, many well-intentioned ministries never get off the ground. Others may successfully form an organization, but fail a short time later if they have not planned ahead.

As I met more and more ministry leaders, I began to see the terrible cost of ministry failure. Then God gave me a vision for helping ministries succeed. In 1999, I left my job at Park Avenue to help found the Faith Communities Project, an effort to build the management skills of ministry leaders. The project is a collaboration of the Center for Nonprofit Management at the University of St. Thomas and TURN (Twin Cities Urban Reconciliation Network). Our first product is a training program called Vision to Reality, which helps ministries address key management issues such as fundraising and financial management. At the time of this book's publication, nearly 100 ministry leaders (many of them from church-based nonprofits) have graduated from the program.

I wrote this book to give church-based nonprofits a better chance at success. The success of these groups is, ultimately, about getting new ministries started to meet real needs in our communities. Success means that churches are better able to reach outside their four walls, extending their ministries beyond the "usual suspects" in the pews and out into the neighborhoods, towns, counties, states, and nations.

For me, the work of helping form church-based nonprofits is all about stories. Stories of God's calling, God's provision, and of the incredible things that happen when we combine the vision and commitment of the church with the resources of the broader community. While my book is full of instructions and worksheets, know that in my heart I feel that this work is all about miracles. I hope my book will lead you to experience some miracles of your own as you move forward with your ministry dream.

Acknowledgments

A number of pastors and ministry leaders agreed to let me interview them for this book. Without exception, they all wanted to share their experiences so that others could benefit:

Rev. Marque Jensen, Cross Connections
    North Minneapolis Christian Fellowship, Minneapolis

Rev. Sunny Kang, Woodland United Methodist Church, Duluth
    and Partnership Advocate, Self Development of People Committee,
    PCUSA

Rev. Austin Kaufmann, The Saint Paul Covenant
    First Covenant Church, Saint Paul

Mary Nelson, Bethel New Life, Chicago

Rev. Cheryl Sanders, Third Street Church of God, Washington, D.C.

John Sommerville, Wooddale Center
    Wooddale Church, Eden Prairie, Minnesota

Trish Vanni, The Leaven Center, Eden Prairie, Minnesota

Sherry Woods, UNIQUE Learning Center, Third Street Church of God,
    Washington, D.C.

I also offer my gratitude to the people of Park Avenue United Methodist Church and the Park Avenue Foundation. Thanks for the joys and challenges of the years I spent working with you. I learned so much! You continue to inspire me.

I am deeply indebted to the two attorneys who worked with me on this book. Eric Skytte of Leonard, Street and Deinard and J. Patrick Plunkett of Moore, Costello & Hart share their considerable gifts with the people of the nonprofit sector every day. My three manuscript readers, Rev. Marchelle Hallman, Rev. Austin Kaufmann, and Trish Vanni, provided invaluable advice on the editing of this book.

The staff at the University of St. Thomas, particularly Patty Wilder, has been a tremendous support to me. And my colleagues at TURN, especially Sheila Ford, Dawn Corlew, and Ann Oliver, have prayed and prayed me through this project. And thank you, Curtiss DeYoung, for freely sharing your ministry contacts.

The graduates of the Vision to Reality training program are like a cheering section for me in my work with congregations. Thanks for showing me that taking risks for God is its own reward. And thanks for being willing to be "guinea pigs" for all of our newest training ideas.

My kind and relentless editor, Beth Ann Gaede, encouraged me and spurred me on to greater excellence.

Pat Peterson, my boss, mentor, and friend, was the most important person to me outside of my family as I worked on this book. Pat was one of the first people to encourage me to take the tremendous step of writing the book, and her encouragement along the way helped keep me focused on the final goal. Pat, the graceful way you live out your faith every day teaches me how to be a Christian woman in the world.

Finally, and most importantly, I could not have completed this book without the support of my family. My husband, Brad Schrag, shared my vision for this book and has supported me in every way. Thanks, Brad, for creating space and time for me to do the work. And my little boy Ethan gave up time with his mama and did not complain when he could not play computer games because I was busy working. My wonderful family spurs me on to a greater vision and supports me as I work to realize my own ministry dream.

Why Should We Start a Nonprofit?
The Advantages and Risks

"God has given me a vision for a transitional housing program," the woman told me, and her eyes lit up as she said it. She wanted to minister to people with the kinds of addictions she had struggled with herself— and conquered. Her pastor encouraged her to dream big about her ministry idea, and she began by identifying an apartment building where she could locate the program. The landlord wanted $200,000 for the building.

It became clear as she began talking to possible funders that they wouldn't give money to the program if it was part of the church. Funders were concerned that a church-based program would be evangelistic or would force people to convert. So she talked with church leaders and convinced them that a separate nonprofit organization was needed in order to attract outside funds.

She struggled through the legal paperwork for months and finally found an attorney who would help her for free. She was surprised by the fees charged by the Internal Revenue Service and had to spend some time raising money to cover about $500 in expenses for incorporating the nonprofit. She recruited three people for the board of the nonprofit—herself, the attorney, and the pastor of the church. The dream seemed within reach.

Once her organization had been approved as an official nonprofit, she quit her "day job" and secured some donated office space, where she set up a phone line. She had business cards printed up for the new program, and began networking in the community. She made some initial inquiries about funding, but funders expressed concern about the lack of a specific plan for implementing the program. It was unclear to them exactly what the program would accomplish, how participants would be recruited, and where the funding and volunteers would come from.

Six months later, after she was unable to raise any funds for the project, she closed down the office and returned to her regular job.

I wish I could tell you that the above story is a fabrication, but it is not. I have worked with many congregations that have pursued setting up a nonprofit by just "falling into" it. It is not unusual for churches to move ahead without much of a plan and without considering the advantages and the risks of setting up a nonprofit. Just "falling into" establishing a new organization is not a very wise approach. It will take you longer to launch the organization and its programs, and you will not be as able to avoid potential pitfalls along the way.

This book will provide you with the stories of success and struggle of congregations working to form their own nonprofits. My own experience comes from serving as executive director of the Park Avenue Foundation, the nonprofit connected to Park Avenue United Methodist Church in South Minneapolis. In addition, I have worked with over 50 other church congregations, providing advice and counsel as they made their way through this process.

I can tell you from my own experience that thorough planning before you form your nonprofit can make all the difference in the success of it. Clarify your mission, your structure, and your program plans early on. If you are not intentional as you move forward, you will be creating unnecessary challenges for yourself. For example, I have worked with congregations that did not discuss how much control the church would have before they set up the nonprofit. As a result, the relationship between the church and the nonprofit started off on a sour note, with church leaders expecting one thing and nonprofit leaders expecting something else entirely.

New organizations have enough struggles overcoming external forces, such as funding trends and community response. You want to eliminate as many internal barriers as possible, so you are ready to face the "outside world." Do not be your own worst enemy! Before you begin to set up your nonprofit, consider the advantages and the risks of this structure.

Advantages:
A Structure That Can Make
Your Ministry Dream Come True

Let us start off with the advantages of forming a separate nonprofit. They are considerable, and in my experience they typically outweigh the risks, depending on the situation at a particular church. Setting up a nonprofit at your church can bring together the very best aspects of the church with the outside resources that a nonprofit can draw.

Congregations bring a great deal to the relationship. Churches frequently have the trust of the broader community in ways that few other institutions do. Particularly if your ministry dream is to offer social service programs, the nonprofit's connection to the church may help you draw participants who would not feel as safe approaching a secular nonprofit, a government agency, or a school.

Churches also have "captive audiences." A congregation is a ready-made group of workers, donors, and supporters. If you prepare them, communicate with them, and inspire them, your congregation can exponentially increase the power of your nonprofit ministry.

When I served as executive director of the Park Avenue Foundation, the congregation of Park Avenue Methodist Church served as a core group of volunteers for foundation programs. Volunteer tutors, mentors, lawyers, doctors, and nurses were all mobilized from within the congregation to do good works every day of the week in the church building. I believe their connection to the church made many of the volunteers more dedicated—they were proud of their church and wanted to ensure that the programs offered were of high quality.

The nonprofit part of the structure (as described below) adds to the organization's effectiveness too. You will be able to attract resources from funders who would not support a church directly. New collaborative partners will become interested in what you are doing, and there will be opportunities to recruit volunteers from new sources. One of the most important advantages is the ability to attract the skills you need through new staff and board members from outside your church.

Advantage 1:
New financial resources can be secured.

Securing new financial resources for ministry is the most common reason that congregations choose to set up a nonprofit. If your ministry needs financial resources from outside your church, having a separate nonprofit will almost certainly aid you in your effort. Of course, you will have to ask for the money! (See chapter 10 on fundraising.) The importance of asking might seem self-evident, but I have worked with several congregations that believed that simply setting up the nonprofit would cause the money to flow in. Some of them are still waiting!

Many foundations, corporations, and government entities will not make grants to congregations directly—with some, it is a stated policy. Other funders have no formal policy against this, but they are uncomfortable giving to religious groups because of fears that contributions for one purpose may be used for something else entirely. Funders might worry that their gift for a church-based job training program might be spent on Sunday school curriculum or choir robes, for example.

Even Christian funders might feel uncomfortable about giving directly to your church. When the Leaven Center, a lay ministry development organization launched by Pax Christi Catholic Community, began fundraising, executive director Trish Vanni said they "absolutely hit the wall with funders. We were not incorporated as a nonprofit yet, and it was clear we were not going to get any gifts from anybody until we took that step. One benefactor who is very interested in our work said 'How do I know my money isn't going to go for stained-glass windows?' The idea of writing out a check to our church that would be deposited in church accounts made him very uncomfortable."

A separate legal entity with its own set of books, governance structure, and board members from outside the church will make many funders much more comfortable about giving to a program connected with a church.

Advantage 2:
New volunteers can be drawn into the ministry.

Having a separate nonprofit allows you to recruit new volunteers from organizations that might be reluctant to send people out to a church.

Many churches I have worked with found they could recruit volunteers for community programs and services much more readily from other churches, local businesses, corporations, or service clubs once they had set up their nonprofit. This is because outside groups are more willing to devote "people power" to programs that are set up to benefit the community, not just the members of one congregation.

I have personally worked with corporations, for example, that send out large groups of volunteers to local nonprofits but would never send volunteers to churches. In Minneapolis, corporate volunteers tutor and mentor children, provide job training, and build new housing, among many other projects. In my experience, you will be better able to tap into corporate volunteers through a separate nonprofit.

Having more organizations to recruit from will also allow you to draw in a greater diversity of volunteers—men and women, and people of different ethnic backgrounds and ages, for example. This diversity of involvement can make your planning processes more representative of the community and therefore more attractive to funders.

Advantage 3:
People with the needed expertise can be recruited.

A new nonprofit with its own staff members and board can help you draw in people with the particular skills that are needed by the ministry. Church boards or councils are composed of representatives from the congregation with a wholistic focus on the faith community. Developing a separate board for the nonprofit will allow you to draw together a wider range of people from the community with the management and fundraising skills you need, rather than living with whoever happens to be on the church board at the time (see chapter 7: Structuring Your Board of Directors). If you are pursuing a day care ministry, for example, you might want a board member who has expertise in day care management, or who is knowledgeable and connected enough to help you get the zoning variance you need through the city council approval process. Board members who work for major corporations could help secure a grant through the corporate giving program.

The ministries under your nonprofit might also require staff people with different types of experience and training than a church could typically attract. A typical church congregation draws employees with experience in teaching, preaching, children's and youth ministry, and worship (to name a few). Depending on the ministries your nonprofit decides to pursue, it may need employees who have entirely different kinds of skills and experiences. You may need social workers, fundraisers, housing and day care specialists, or chemical dependency counselors, for example. You may also decide to hire an executive director for the nonprofit.

Even if you want to hire people of faith for all positions, you may need to go outside your own congregation to find the best candidates. Employees coming from a different denominational perspective may be more comfortable being employed by a nonprofit than a church of a "different flavor." Potential employees may also be more likely to be drawn to an organization with board members and supervisory staff who have knowledge in the field in which they work—family counseling or housing, for example. If there are other experts in their field within the organization, employees may have greater opportunities to build their own skills through training, mentoring, and new program development.

Advantage 4:
New collaborative partnerships will become possible.

Having a separate nonprofit will help you collaborate with some organizations that would be reluctant to partner directly with a church. From my experience, government agencies, public schools, and neighborhood groups seem particularly cautious about alliances with churches. When a group of like-minded people get together to address a community issue, for example, coming under the banner of the nonprofit might make others at the table less suspicious of your motives for involvement. Some people automatically assume that the hidden agenda behind any congregational involvement is recruiting new church members. If your separate nonprofit has the mission of "alleviating substandard housing in the central neighborhood," for example, it makes your purpose clear and shows others that you are willing to devote time and resources to a community issue that others care about as well.

Advantage 5:
Decisions can be made more rapidly.

Let's face it: most congregations are not known for their speedy and efficient decision-making processes. Sometimes this is unavoidable; for example, your denomination might require you to discuss decisions at a certain number of meetings or notify the congregation well in advance that a vote will be taken at a particular time.

Take an honest look at your congregation's decision-making processes. If they are so lengthy and complex that they derail ministry ideas, setting up a nonprofit may be a way to help new ministry "hatch" more quickly. This will be particularly important if you are considering new ministry in which decisions are time sensitive. Housing ministries frequently need to buy property quickly when the opportunity arises, for example. Opportunities to apply for large grants or to pursue a new collaboration may require you to make decisions in a much shorter time frame as well.

One leader of a church-based nonprofit said: "Not being part of the annual planning and budgeting cycle of the church has given us more latitude on how we design and move. We can be more highly entrepreneurial, step into new opportunities, find funds for them, shift gears, or shut something down. We have more freedom and can be more spontaneous in responding to opportunities."

Advantage 6:
The nonprofit can be insulated from the politics and personalities of the church.

Many people find it difficult to talk about the hard truths of church politics—and it may be hard to read this, particularly if you are a pastor. Here it is: the political culture that evolves in some churches can hinder ministry rather than help it. If you are in a church setting in which a small handful of people (they could be staff, board members, or vocal congregation members) have gained considerable power and use it to manipulate people and situations, creating a separate nonprofit could give you the chance to start over with new people who will create a new culture. So rather than focusing on "what Ed wants" or "what Ed will go along with," you can focus your energy on what is best for the ministry. This does not mean that you will not have to deal with Ed or his friends at all, but a separate organization can help insulate ministry from some of the political aspects of the church.

Advantage 7:
The nonprofit can better pursue potentially controversial ministries.

Some churches set up nonprofits to pursue potentially controversial ministries that the church would be more reluctant to develop. An example would be a justice ministry that "takes on city hall" using a confrontational approach to bring about positive community change. This is one of the reasons First Covenant Church in St. Paul developed their nonprofit, The Saint Paul Covenant. The church is located in a neighborhood and a city where political confrontation seems to be necessary in getting just about anything done. Church leaders recognized that congregation members might be uncomfortable working in this system, although some confrontation would be required to meet the church's mission of pursuing justice issues.

According to the Reverend Austin Kaufmann, executive director of the St. Paul Covenant and pastor of congregational life at the church, the nonprofit was "formed with an understanding that compassion needs hands and justice needs a backbone, which at times is conflictual for a church to do based on faith or theological positions."

Bringing in more controversial or "on the edge" speakers for special events might also be easier for the nonprofit to do; for example, the church might be uncomfortable aligning itself with someone who has a strikingly different theology from the pastoral staff. Having the nonprofit host the speaker instead gives the church some room to say, "This isn't our program!"

One church-based nonprofit leader I spoke with put it this way: "Having the nonprofit gives our denominational leader and the leaders of our church room to be proud of what they like. It also gives them a ready way to distance themselves from us if what we are doing is over the line."

Advantage 8:
Insulate the church from legal liability or financial responsibility for ministry under the nonprofit.

If you set up your nonprofit as an entirely separate entity (with the church exercising very little if any control over it), it can help insulate the church from legal claims arising out of the programs under the nonprofit's umbrella. Attorneys I have worked with tell me that in order for this to work, the nonprofit has to operate very independently from the church. The bylaws, articles of incorporation, board structure, and staffing for the nonprofit must all be set up so that the church has very limited control.

This insulation from liability will be particularly beneficial if the nonprofit is pursuing new ministry in which there is greater risk of lawsuits; for example, a youth-adult mentoring program or a camping ministry in which youth will be canoeing or rock climbing. Having the nonprofit will not eliminate the need for risk management procedures or adequate planning, however. All ministry leaders have the duty to ensure that volunteers and participants are as safe as can be at all times.

Having a nonprofit can also help insulate the church from being entirely responsible for the financial state of programs under the nonprofit umbrella. This can be a real benefit if you are pursuing a ministry dream with some significant financial risks. Churches that have a passion for purchasing and renovating housing in their neighborhood, for example, are undertaking something that may have large and hidden costs. If you have ever been involved in construction, you know that it usually costs more than you thought. In this situation, a nonprofit operating independently of the church would keep these large expenses from cutting into the budget for core church ministry areas such as worship, Sunday school, and the music program.

The Risks of Having a Nonprofit

There are some real risks to setting up a nonprofit at a church as well. Compared with other nonprofit structures, this sort of alliance has added complexity. You could look at it almost like a merger of two organizations: one old (the church) and one new (the nonprofit). You are founding a group with a new vision and drawing in new people and resources to move that vision forward. At the same time, you do not want the people of the church to feel disconnected from the nonprofit, so you will need to work to help them feel a sense of ownership for it. Depending on your denomination, you may also need to develop this new organization within a framework of existing rules and expectations. Whew! It is possible to keep this all in balance, but it can be difficult. So, as you are going through the process, if it seems hard, that's because it is!

If you do not pay attention to some of the risks described below, the resulting conflict can hinder your ministry. You will be spending more time negotiating with staff and resolving conflicts than you ever expected. This is time taken away from the important tasks of forming a new organization and hatching new ministry.

Most of the problems I describe here come down to interpersonal relationships. When you separate part of your ministry into another organization, there is much greater room for misunderstanding among the people involved. This greater risk of misunderstanding occurs, in part, because the key players will not all be sitting at the same table (literally or figuratively) as often as they did before. All of that regular communication that just occurred as a matter of course at staff and board meetings probably will not happen as frequently. You will have to be much more deliberate about keeping each other "in the loop." Keep investing time in communicating with people regularly and respectfully, and it will pay off in the short-term and the long-term (see chapter 11: Maintaining a Positive Relationship with Your Church).

Special Risks

Now might not be the right time to set up a nonprofit if any of the following is true for your church. This is not to say that you must rule out a nonprofit forever, but it might be good to wait until the congregation has more stability or fewer factions before you proceed.

1. Significant Church Staff or Board Transitions

Churches that are undergoing significant transitions on their staff or boards may want to delay setting up a nonprofit. If your senior pastor or another key staff member is moving on, or if there has been significant turnover on your church board, you may not have the strong support among key leaders that you need to move forward.

2. A Recent Breach of Trust within the Church

People who are working together to spin off a whole new organization have to trust each other. If there has recently been a split in your church, or if something has happened that makes the congregation suspicious of new ideas or new people, you may need to wait for some healing to take place before you move ahead.

3. Significant Factions or Conflict in the Congregation

All churches experience conflict, but there are some churches that have a culture of constant conflict. If your church usually breaks into "us and them" factions around key ministry issues, this could hinder your ability to develop a nonprofit. If you decide to go ahead, you will need a strong facilitator and some ground rules for how people who disagree will be expected to interact with each other. Also, work to engage people of differing perspectives in the planning process for the nonprofit.

Risk 1:
The nonprofit may become disconnected from the mission of the church.

It is possible that the nonprofit could veer off in a different direction than the church, particularly if the church decides not to exercise much control over the new organization's mission or governance. The group that was formed to help fulfill part of the church's mission now seems to be doing something totally different than what it was set up to do. For example, the church's mission is place specific—"we're anchored in the Bancroft neighborhood"—and the nonprofit is looking at setting up programming in a nearby suburb. The difference might also be about the type of ministry that is being pursued or the way in which it is implemented.

One church I worked with had a nonprofit focused on community ministry that was run by a strong president and a small group of volunteers. The church's vision was for "equipping of the saints" within their congregation—for as many church members as possible to be developing ministry and volunteering in the community. This was not the vision of the president of the nonprofit and his board, however, who were moving the nonprofit more and more toward paid, professional staff positions and corporate partnerships. The church wanted a fully engaged congregation, and the nonprofit leadership wanted to focus on external resources and partners. These two visions could have worked together, but a breakdown in communication brought everything to an impasse. The president of the nonprofit eventually left his position over the issue.

Risk 2:
The ministry can lose its faith focus.

Forming a nonprofit could diminish the faith focus of the ministries under its umbrella. If the church serves as the spiritual "engine" for ministry, then distance from it might make faith a minor part of the nonprofit's work rather than the driving force behind it. Sometimes this occurs because the nonprofit draws in people and funders who share the vision for the community but not necessarily the faith aspect of it.

Here is a possible scenario: The church founds the nonprofit to serve the people of the community and to "share the love of Jesus Christ." As time goes on, however, the nonprofit receives grants from foundations and government that cannot be used for spiritual aspects of the program. Also, a number of people from outside the church fill the nonprofit board. Over time, if there is not a strong connection with the church, the nonprofit may want to remove some of the spiritual language from its mission statement in order to attract more secular funders or partners.

Of course, if your congregation wants to launch a nonprofit that has a very limited faith focus or none at all, this is not a risk you need to worry about.

Risk 3:
The church may assume less ownership for the ministry.

One of the risks of having a nonprofit is that church members can more easily say, "That's the nonprofit's responsibility; they don't need my money or time for the ministry." If church members see that the nonprofit is successful at securing outside funding or bringing in outside volunteers, they might assume that their help is not needed. Though it might be possible for you to secure enough outside resources to run the nonprofit, you can probably do more and higher quality ministry when you add the people and financial resources of the church to the mix.

A communication plan that keeps the work of the nonprofit constantly before the congregation will help. It should include a strategy of asking church members for both their money and their time. Let your church members know they are needed.

Risk 4:
Having a nonprofit costs more than not having one.

Having a nonprofit costs more than not having one, regardless of how you set it up. If you pursue new staff members to manage the organization and its programs, it will cost more for salaries and benefits. Program supplies and transportation costs will likely be higher. Even if staff time, facility use, and a number of other expenses are donated by the church, it will still cost you more to have a nonprofit; for example, there are filing fees to maintain your nonprofit status, letterhead and brochures to print, more postage, and additional insurance expenses. Consider these additional expenses as you decide whether to set up the nonprofit.

Risk 5:
Tension could develop between the nonprofit and church leaders and staff.

Setting up a separate nonprofit may make church staff and lay leaders feel suspicious—as though a separate group of people is going off to do their "own thing" apart from the church. There may also be some hurt feelings—

a sense of "why didn't they give us a chance to do this ministry within the church. Do they think we're not capable?" Of course, the "us and them" view of the process can be mitigated if you develop the nonprofit with the strong input of church staff and leaders. Even if you do not implement all of the suggestions that are made, seeking out their opinions will make church staff and lay leaders feel a sense of ownership in the process and will help them have a more positive view of the nonprofit.

One group I worked with formed a nonprofit without much input from church staff and church board members. "It was a small group of church council members that worked on developing the nonprofit, and it was never completely represented to the church staff," the executive director of the nonprofit explained. "This led a number of staff to mistrust the nonprofit from the outset. Within a couple of years, all of the members of the council that had helped start the nonprofit had rotated off, so there were no 'true believers' left there. If I had it to do over, I would include our church members and staff in a brainstorming session about forming the nonprofit. The broader the buy-in and ownership the better."

Risk 6:
The nonprofit will create more administrative work.

Once your nonprofit is formed, there will simply be more to do administratively. There will be more paperwork, more programs to be overseen, more meetings to be planned and held, and potentially more staff to be supervised. If you secure funding from foundation or government sources, there will be grants and reports to be written on a regular basis.

The administrative aspect is often an afterthought for churches. Ministry leaders are so busy delivering the ministry that they forget the planning and administration that needs to go on behind the scenes to make it all happen. These administrative functions are just as critical to ministry success as finding the right youth worker or preaching the right sermon. Even the best-planned event cannot succeed if the mailing does not go out on time!

Pulling off these additional administrative pieces may be more difficult for smaller churches with limited staffing available. It may also be difficult for churches that are not gifted in this area. If you have difficulty now planning board meetings, sending out mailings, supervising staff, or organizing programs, forming a nonprofit will only add to this burden. Of course, this can be an advantage to forming a nonprofit too—you can add administratively gifted staff members on the nonprofit side to effectively manage those aspects of the work.

Risk 7:
You will have to raise funds.

Once you form your nonprofit, the organization will need to devote energy and time to the task of fundraising. Writing grants and building relationships with funders takes a great deal of time, and these fundraising tasks may pull you away from developing programs or other aspects of your organization. Keep in mind that it almost always takes longer than you think it will to secure your first grants, particularly if you are starting from scratch with a new nonprofit and a new program vision (most funders like to see a track record).

"Sometimes I wish we didn't have to spend so much time raising money for our nonprofit," one leader told me. "If this was a part of the church budget, there would be a broader constituency figuring it out and providing support every year." Another leader of a church nonprofit said that her group had been able to secure a $40,000 grant from city government, but she estimated that their nonprofit devoted about $40,000 worth of staff time to completing reporting requirements and maintaining relationships with city staff.

One way to build your nonprofit's fundraising capacity from the outset is for the church to provide some "seed money" for start-up fundraising costs. A fundraising consultant or grant writer could be hired to seek funds while other aspects of the organization are being put into place.

A Checklist

The Advantages and Risks of Setting Up a Nonprofit at Our Church

Use the following checklist to help you identify the advantages and risks that would be present in your situation.

Reasons to Form a Nonprofit

Check all that apply.

To pursue our ministry dream we need to form a nonprofit because:

_____ We need outside funding, and these funders will not give directly to the church.

_____ We need to attract staff members or board members from outside our church to bring needed expertise.

_____ We need more volunteers for the nonprofit's programs than our church can provide.

_____ The collaborative partners we need to work with would not partner directly with the church.

_____ Our dream is for a potentially controversial ministry that the church itself would be uncomfortable launching.

_____ The new ministry has financial and legal risks that the church needs to be insulated from.

_____ Our church culture (its pace and its politics) would make it difficult to develop the new ministry.

Risks of setting up a nonprofit at our church

Check all that apply.

We might want to wait to form our nonprofit or consider an alternative structure because:

_____ We are concerned that the nonprofit will become disconnected from the mission of the church.

_____ We are concerned that ministries set up under the nonprofit will lose their faith focus.

_____ We are not equipped to undertake the administrative or fundraising burdens of a separate nonprofit.

_____ There is not enough support from key church staff and lay leaders for the formation of the nonprofit.

_____ We do not have the funds we need for start-up expenses of the nonprofit.

_____ We are concerned that our church members will lose their sense of ownership for any ministries set up under the nonprofit.

_____ Our congregation is undergoing significant transition in staff or board positions.

_____ People in our congregation do not trust each other right now because of a recent conflict or problem in the church.

Addressing the Risks

Checking off one or more of the risks listed above does not mean that your congregation should never pursue setting up a nonprofit. It might simply mean that you need to wait until the congregation has come out of a transition time, or that you need to do more planning around some issues. For example, if starting the nonprofit is critical to realizing your ministry dream (see chapter 2), then you need to find ways to develop more administrative capacity, or raise some start-up money, or find a way to ensure that the nonprofit will keep its faith focus.

All of the risks and advantages above are addressed in this book. My hope is that you will use this book to help plan the process of forming your nonprofit, which will help you realize the advantages of this structure and avoid pitfalls along the way.

2

Realizing Your Ministry Dream:
The One Reason to Pursue
the Formation of a Nonprofit

"Our church is in a financial bind—we can't make our mortgage payment or cover the pastor's salary. If we set up a nonprofit, we'll be able to get foundation grants for those expenses."

"We want to partner with Firstcorp, so we'll set up a nonprofit to do it."

"We want a nonprofit because all of the other churches in our denomination have one."

"We want a nonprofit because it's a sign of a successful church."

I hear these statements so frequently as I work with congregations, and they always give me pause. While the possibility of new money, new partnerships, and new visibility may be attractive to your church, there is only one thing that should drive the formation of a nonprofit: your ministry dream cannot succeed without it. I cannot stress this enough. If you let what is best for the ministry drive the decision-making process around forming a nonprofit, there will be less conflict and more buy-in by your congregation and leaders. Also, the ministry that eventually develops under the nonprofit's umbrella will be more successful.

Unfortunately, churches often focus on everything except the ministry dream when pursuing this process. The promise of securing new money and corporate partnerships frequently drives the formation of a church-based nonprofit. External resources can lend a real boost to a ministry, but resources pumped into a poorly formed ministry vision won't bring the results you seek. It is dangerous to let money become the primary driving force within your organization, because you will have plenty of opportunities to compromise your mission in order to get the money.

Decision-Making Patterns
That Develop in Churches

I am advising you to cling to your ministry dream as the driving force in this process because churches often develop decision-making norms that focus on something unrelated to helping the ministry. It is important to be aware of this tendency to lose focus on the dream so you can spot it when it happens and respond accordingly. Imagine you are sitting at a church board meeting and you raise the issue of forming a nonprofit. The first time you bring it up, you might hear responses such as:

- "This is too risky. We just don't know what will happen."
- "It will cost too much money."
- "A church six blocks down the street did this and it was a disaster. The nonprofit went off on its own and now it doesn't even have a faith focus."
- "We can pursue this new ministry with the church staff. I don't know why we need a whole new organization."
- "We've always done things this way."
- "Ed won't like this at all."

If you start with the ministry dream instead, you will have a better chance of diffusing some of the usual decision-making roadblocks. If your congregation is truly ignited by the dream, they will look for ways to make it happen, instead of finding ways to stop it.

Fully Developing the Ministry Dream

A ministry dream is not just a mission statement; it is a very specific passion for service. You can see what your fully realized dream looks like when you close your eyes. Depending on what your dream is, when you close your eyes you might see:

- people who are healthy instead of sick
- church members who are equipped to preach, teach, and serve the community
- a crime-free community where there is affordable housing for everyone
- 100 new churches planted within the next 10 years
- youth who graduate from high school and go to college

Many books have been written about the proper way to write vision and mission statements, but I want to focus here on the "dream" aspect of developing new ministry, because I think in a church setting, it is what drives people forward. I believe that if God's people can see the promise of what God calls us to—the beauty of the "end result" rather than just the hard work—we will be willing to undertake just about anything.

If a congregation "sees" the ministry dream together, then the energy for it multiplies exponentially. It becomes part of the story of the group, and what we say to each other and do together reinforces how important the ministry dream is to all of us. When we worship, have meetings, get together to study God's Word, and socialize, we all talk about the dream because it is something we share.

While I served as executive director of the Park Avenue Foundation, the public school system began testing students for reading and math skills. The newspaper published a list of all of the schools in the state, ranking them based on how well their students did on the test. The public school located just three blocks from the church was at the very bottom of the list in reading scores! A core group of congregation members and church staff got together and said: "We can't just do nothing. This is our community and these are our kids." The energy of this small group of people, as well as some well-placed communication from the pulpit, led to the formation of Building Up Reading Skills through Tutoring (BURSTT), a tutoring program that provides volunteer tutors for kids every week to improve reading skills. Over the years, hundreds of students have participated in the program. This all happened because the congregation grabbed hold of a clearly expressed ministry dream: "All of the children in our community should be able to read."

Where the Ministry Dream Comes From

Some churches expect their pastor to tell them what the ministry dream is, but from my experience, it can come from many different places and from many different types of people within a church.

One of my favorite stories is about a nonprofit formed out of the outrageous act of faith committed by one member of Pax Christi Catholic Community in Eden Prairie, Minnesota. A man who served on the maintenance staff at the church met a young couple who needed a stove. In response to their need, he went into the church kitchen, unhooked the stove, and gave it to them.

Word got out that the staff member had done this. Some people within the parish were upset, but at the same time, everyone realized that this was the kind of courageous act of faith that Pax Christi was encouraging its members to take. Once people in the church heard about the stove, they began to donate their own used furniture and household items. Soon the maintenance room at the church was "filled to the gills" with items donated by church members. The spontaneous act of generosity by one person evolved into a ministry called Bridging, Inc., which now has a 4,000 square-foot warehouse and provides furniture and household items to 75 families each week.

Take a look at the following list and see where you think the ministry dream comes from in your congregation:

The mission statement of your church may move you forward into ministry that could best be accomplished within a separate nonprofit.

North Minneapolis Christian Fellowship is a congregation that is dedicated to racial reconciliation and community development within the Jordan neighborhood of North Minneapolis. The church's formal mission statement is "to speak the words and do the works of Jesus." The church was founded in 1991 with a "planting philosophy" that included the formation of a nonprofit called Cross Connections to focus on community development.

Co-pastor Marque Jensen said the nonprofit "is about fulfilling the second part of our church mission—'the works of Jesus.' Our nonprofit builds connections and networks in the community . . . to help people overcome barriers in their lives. We say that Cross Connections is about "bridging the gaps with love." The nonprofit sponsors a job-training program and is developing both a charter school and an apartment complex for low-income seniors.

Your pastor may have a ministry dream that spurs you to develop a nonprofit.

Often, God calls pastors to a prophetic, visionary role that can spur the rest of the congregation into action. Your pastor may have a picture or vision of all that the church body could do if only they took steps forward in faith. Forming a nonprofit might be necessary to capture and develop your pastor's "God-sized" visions.

The late Rev. Samuel Hines of Third Street Church of God in Washington, D.C., had a God-sized vision for a reconciliation and community development ministry that drove the development of a separate nonprofit called United Neighbors Involved in Quality Urban Experience (UNIQUE). UNIQUE pursued the development of "Reconciliation Square," a "Tabernacle of Witness" in the nation's capital. The plans for the new ministry included an apartment complex, community center, conference center, and hotel on the blocks adjacent to the church. Its purpose was to "build a model community based upon the reconciliation concept."

While this vision has not yet been fully realized, Third Street Church of God continues to be active in community development and reconciliation 91 years after its founding. The UNIQUE Learning Center (organized under another church-affiliated nonprofit called One Ministries) provides after-school programming every day to students in kindergarten through grade 12 from the community, as well as a career internship program for older youth. The program has helped many young people succeed in school and go on to college.

A passage of Scripture may lead your church to develop its ministry dream.

Bethel New Life, Inc., a nonprofit founded by Bethel Lutheran Church on the West Side of Chicago, has chosen a Scripture passage as its mission statement:

"If you put an end to oppression, to every gesture of contempt, and to every evil word; if you give food to the hungry and satisfy those who are in need, then the darkness around you will turn to the brightness of noon . . . your people will rebuild what has been in ruins, building again on the old foundations. You will be known as the people who rebuilt the walls, who restored the ruined houses" (excerpt from Isa. 58:9-12).

This passage is the motivating force behind the ministries of Bethel New Life, and leads them to develop housing programs, senior services, job training, and many other services that help "rebuild the walls" in the neighborhood. The mission statement has also challenged the organization to "build on the old foundations," drawing on the assets of the people and institutions that are in the neighborhood. Bethel New Life has resisted giving up its scriptural mission statement, even when secular funders have expressed discomfort with it.

The history of your congregation may inspire you and spur you on to greater action in a particular ministry area.

By looking back at your church's past, you may find the inspiration to move forward into new ministry. The heroic acts of your congregation's founders, a key pastor, or a group of lay leaders may almost become part of the "legend" of the church, even if your congregation is relatively young.

One church I have worked with fought hard to racially integrate itself in the 1950s when African American families first began to move into its all-white neighborhood. There was controversy within the church over inviting African American families into the congregation, and while a number of white families left at the time, the church continues to be one of the few churches in its city where a significant number of both white and black families worship together on a Sunday morning.

This history has inspired this church to reach out to the many Latino families now moving into its community. The church has taken several concrete steps that include offering a bilingual Sunday morning service and featuring Latino speakers and music groups in its annual outdoor festival.

Small groups within a church may "bubble up" with ministry ideas.

Sometimes the dream comes from a group of people within the church. They might be in a small group Bible study or volunteer together in a ministry. I witnessed this many times while at Park Avenue Church. One year the physicians and healthcare workers in the congregation got together to talk about starting a health clinic at the church. The excitement of this small group of people led to the development of the Park Avenue/St. Mary's Clinic, which provides free basic health care to people without health insurance. The clinic was housed under the umbrella of the Park Avenue Foundation and is a partnership with Carondelet Lifecare, a ministry of the Sisters of St. Joseph of Carondelet, an order of Catholic nuns.

There are so many wonderful traditions within the Christian church that you may have an entirely different way of discerning your ministry dream than the ones described in this chapter. Be sure to take the time to reflect on your own traditions and theologies, so that you can develop a way of clarifying the ministry dream that best suits your congregation.

Elements of a Ministry Dream

Putting your ministry dream into a simple but compelling statement can help you gain support for the dream and the formation of your nonprofit.

The following is a list of sample ministry dream statements:

- New immigrants will feel welcome in our community.
- All of the children in our community will read at their grade level.
- Young adults ages 18 through 35 will be drawn into a relationship with Jesus Christ and the church.
- There will be enough safe, affordable housing for everyone in our community.

In my experience, great ministry dreams have certain characteristics.

- **Great ministry dreams are focused on how people's lives will be changed.**
  It is easy to write down a list of programs that we will "do"; it is even harder to think in terms of the ultimate impact we want to have through our actions. Running a medical clinic is not a ministry dream; however, ensuring that all people in your community have access to quality health care is. Keep asking yourself: "How will people's lives be transformed as a result of our ministry?"
- **Great ministry dreams are too big to accomplish, maybe even in our lifetimes.**

Dreams need to be big in order to be inspiring, and a dream that is challenging can draw the best out of everyone. Also, big dreams can provide opportunities for a larger group of people to be involved, since you will need the talents and willingness of more than a few to realize the dream.

- **Great ministry dreams have a specific "outcome."**
Make sure there is a "what" in your ministry dream. Many churches fall into the trap of focusing on "meeting all of the needs of our community." Even if that is not your stated mission or dream, your congregation could drift in that direction if you are not more focused. "Ensuring that all community residents are productive" is too broad to be an effective dream. "All community residents will have safe, affordable housing" narrows the dream down so that you have a specific focus.

- **Great ministry dreams are much more than a list of tasks to do.**
Resist the temptation to write down everything you will "do" in your ministry and use that as your dream. It might be easy for you to write down something like: "We will offer a job training program three days a week." That is your program plan. Your ministry dream would be: "All community residents will be employed at living wage jobs."

Sharing the Ministry Dream

At its best, a ministry dream will run like a thread through everything you say and do as a congregation. If it is fully embraced by your church members, you will be unable to get away from the dream—written materials will refer to it, meetings will be convened around it, sermons will be preached about it, and songs will be sung about it. Perhaps most important, people in the church will talk about it in their conversations with each other.

How do you get the congregation, lay leaders, and key church staff to "catch the ministry dream?" Here are some possible strategies:

- Preach sermons or provide biblical teaching about the ministry dream and its relationship to the church's mission. Having some occasions where the entire congregation hears about it will be important to their ability to understand and embrace it.

- Offer Sunday school sessions or opportunities for small groups to study Scripture passages or a book related to the ministry dream. If your dream is to help alleviate hunger in your community and around the world, you could, for example, read the re-issue of *Rich Christians in an Age of Hunger* by Ron Sider as a congregation or in your small groups.
- Engage a small group of key formal or informal church leaders in a planning process about "catching the dream," so that key steps to moving forward can be identified and communicated to the congregation.
- Start the ministry on a small scale (a pilot project), and invite members of the church to participate as volunteers early on. The volunteers will be the best salespeople for the ministry dream. Get those volunteers into relationships with kids, the elderly, or new immigrants, for example, and they will be hooked. They may not be able to stop talking about their experiences to their friends at church.
- Use the congregation's regular written materials; for example, make sure the ministry dream is described on the cover of the bulletin or in the church newsletter.
- Create special communication pieces about the ministry dream. A brochure with photos, a special newsletter, or a video might be just what the congregation needs to really grab hold of the dream.

Ministry Dream Worksheet

1. Write down a word picture of your congregation's ministry dream.

    What do you see when you picture your ministry dream?

    Who will participate in it?

    How will people's lives be changed by the ministry?

2. What are the reasons you need a nonprofit in order to realize your ministry dream?

3. Where did the ministry dream come from?

4. Who else needs to buy into the ministry dream before you can move forward? What strategies will you use?

Is Your Congregation Ready?

McNiff Memorial Church is a growing congregation located in Winslow, a town of about 5,000 people located in the middle of the state. The town's population has increased dramatically in the last three years with an influx of Spanish-speaking immigrants, most of whom have come to work at the poultry-processing plant located there. There has been a mixed reaction in the town to the new residents—some people feel nervous about the town being "overrun" by people different than themselves; others feel excited about the chance to build cross-cultural relationships.

The church board chair at McNiff Church as well as three lay people feel passionate about reaching out to the new immigrants and begin to look into ways that this can be accomplished. They form a small task force and decide to connect with a new Spanish-speaking congregation that is meeting in a storefront on Main Street.

At the meeting, the pastor of the Spanish church expresses the need for a new meeting space for their church, as the current space is just too small and provides no room for Sunday school or other programs. He also describes the need that his church members have for health care, English as a Second Language classes, and job training. None of the social service agencies or churches in the area is currently providing these programs for Spanish-speaking people.

The four members of McNiff leave the meeting very excited, and prepare a proposal for the McNiff church board. They recommend that the Spanish-speaking church be allowed to meet at McNiff at 2:00 P.M. every Sunday for their worship service. They also recommend that the church look into forming a nonprofit that would provide health care, education, and training to Spanish-speaking immigrants in their town in collaboration with the Spanish-speaking church.

The McNiff church board chair has contacts with a foundation that makes grants in the county, and he has had a promising conversation about getting funding for the start-up nonprofit. The senior pastor of the church seems less sure about the task force's proposals, because he is not confident that most of the congregation members are supportive of opening their church to the new immigrants. In fact, there are several vocal elderly people in the congregation who are worried about "wear and tear" to the building if so many more people are allowed in on Sunday and during the rest of the week.

Is Our Congregation Ready to Form a Nonprofit?

Almost every congregation I have helped to form a nonprofit has asked me "how do I know when our congregation is ready?" The question is difficult to answer, because there is no set list of things that you need to have before you proceed. Usually, the situation is similar to the one described above— there will be several strong signs to move ahead, and several others that say "stop!" The truth is, every church is different, and even if the only thing you can count on is the support of the senior pastor, sometimes it still means you can and should proceed.

Incidentally, this is different advice than I give to secular organizations. Sometimes we are called in faith to do things that do not seem to make sense or that are not popular with the people around us; however, avoid using this as an excuse for not clarifying your vision, or building the relationships you need with key leaders.

The following checklist is simply meant as a guide. Do not worry if you cannot check them all; however, the more items you check on the list, the easier the launch of the nonprofit will be and the more quickly you will be able to launch new ministry under its umbrella. Many of the issues in the list are addressed in subsequent chapters of this book.

Signs That Your Congregation Is Ready to Form a Nonprofit

_____ We have a ministry dream that cannot be realized without the nonprofit.

Your congregation has caught the vision: to build 20 new units of affordable housing, or to start a welfare-to-work training program. Now what? A key group of leaders from your church should sit down together to define what you need to proceed. The group could include key leaders at the church: pastors, key program staff, and several board members and committee chairs.

Your planning group may sense that the ministry dream needs a partnership with HUD or the pubic schools to succeed. Will these groups partner with a church, or would they be more inclined to connect with a separate nonprofit? Maybe your dream needs the support of all of the churches in the community—both their money and their volunteers. Keeping the ministry dream at least somewhat separate from your church might more readily attract the support of other denominations.

Review the "Reasons to Form a Nonprofit" checklist at the end of chapter 1 to see if your ministry dream needs a nonprofit structure in order to develop and flourish.

_____ We want to develop a ministry that extends beyond the church congregation or the core ministry areas of the church.

When you form the nonprofit, develop a mission for it that will take your church a step further in ministry. For example, the new organization could lead you to try a new ministry or to serve new kinds of people. The mission of the nonprofit should focus on something more than serving your own congregation or developing the core ministry areas of the church. Core ministries are those you would expect a church to offer to its own congregation members, including Sunday school, faith formation or adult education, a youth group or children's church, visitation and hospitality ministries, and basic worship functions such as the church choir. These are ministries that usually exist for the primary benefit of church members, and are generally accepted as something that a church should do for the people who are a part of the congregation.

Sometimes when churches cannot seem to get their act together in their core ministry areas, they decide to put these ministries under the nonprofit. Usually, this is done in an attempt to secure new funding for a core ministry, by somehow working expenses for that ministry into the budget of the nonprofit. I always discourage groups from doing this.

One of the main purposes of spinning off a separate organization is to begin or strengthen ministry that has a focus beyond the four walls of your congregation. Sometimes this means a geographical shift—moving the new ministry out of the church building into the neighborhood or your metropolitan area. Maybe the shift for you will be from local to national, or even international. Or the ministry might remain right in your building but many of the people you are serving will be from outside of your own congregation. The primary work of the nonprofit would be to serve your targeted population rather than to grow your congregation.

It can be difficult to determine what the church should take responsibility for and what could be spun off into the nonprofit. For instance, you may have a youth choir at your church, but if you desire to develop it into a performance troupe that will include youth from outside your church and offer performances around the community, you may want to consider connecting it to the nonprofit in some way. Some churches have done such a good job of developing their own core ministry areas that they have set up a nonprofit to help other churches develop strong ministries too. The Leaven Center at Pax Christi Catholic Community in Eden Prairie, Minnesota, is an example of this, as is the Wooddale Center at Wooddale Church, also in Eden Prairie.

____ The ministry we are proposing is wanted and needed by the community we wish to serve.

How will you find out whether the community wants what you are proposing? Ask them! Ideally, interacting with community members will be an important early step in your discussions about forming the nonprofit (see chapter 4, pp. 41-44).

Getting feedback from your target "customers" is key. If, for example, your dream is to start a job-training program for high school youth, do not start to flesh out the details until you have actually talked to living, breathing teenagers. First, ask them if job training is what they want. If they say yes, ask them what it looks like. Is training offered during the day or at night? What topics should be covered in the classes? Where should you meet? Who should teach? Getting feedback on all of these details will help you develop an effective program. It will also give your customers a sense of ownership in the program.

In addition to talking with your potential customers, be sure to get the input of community leaders. They will also provide invaluable advice that will help you develop your ministry. Formal leaders such as elected officials, the pastors of other churches, and heads of key nonprofits or government agencies can be a great help. You should also try to get a sense of who the informal leaders or elders in your community are and talk with them as well. These folks may not hold a title, but they may be vocal and influential nonetheless.

Understanding the community will help you focus your efforts where they are most needed. Also, the process of asking the community for input will help you build respectful relationships with the people you are trying to serve.

_____ We have defined a clear niche and mission for our proposed nonprofit.

Be clear about what you are trying to accomplish through the nonprofit by working toward a focused mission statement before you launch the organization. If you have a big vision or a community with many needs, it is easy to develop a mission that sounds almost like a "laundry list" of community needs and ministry goals. Instead, go through a planning process (described in chapter 4) that narrows it down. Your mission should identify the following:

- Who are you trying to serve? (Youth, families, people without health insurance?)
- Where are you going to do it? (Your neighborhood, your region, nationally?)
- What are you going to do? (Help people read, provide housing, train pastors of all denominations?)
- How are you going to do it?

You will also need to identify the "niche" of your nonprofit before you launch it. Spend some time researching what other similar organizations in your area are doing and define how your nonprofit's mission is different. Other groups may provide a similar program, but yours will reach a different group of people, or include a new faith focus, or be more intensive. Sometimes many groups need to run similar programs because the need is so great.

If one or more of your focus areas are already being addressed by another organization, this could allow you to focus your efforts in an area in which other organizations are not yet working. For example, if the original vision of your nonprofit is to provide housing and support services to seniors, and you discover that housing needs are being met by other groups, you can focus your mission on providing home health care and chore service instead.

Understanding what other groups are doing could also provide you with some opportunities to collaborate. The possibilities are almost limitless and might include referring clients, sharing staff, curriculum, equipment and space, and applying for grants together. Other organizations could also provide technical assistance to you as you set up your program and nonprofit.

____ The senior pastor of our church supports the development of the nonprofit.

You should not proceed with the formation of a nonprofit without the support of the senior pastor of the church. In some churches and denominations, the senior pastor is the one who carries forward key initiatives—he or she will be the one who will represent this to the church board and congregation and carry it through the approval process. In other churches, the pastor may act as more of a facilitator, encouraging lay leaders to develop and champion new ideas. Regardless of how your pastor operates, he or she must be supportive of the idea of forming a nonprofit if you are to proceed.

While it might be possible for a small group within the church to form a nonprofit without the senior pastor's support, it is not advisable. Proceeding without his or her support can undermine the work of the nonprofit and divide the congregation just when you need people to pull together to launch your new organization.

_____ Other key church staff support the development of the nonprofit.

There are probably people on your church staff who can provide valuable support and insight into the formation of the nonprofit, but they can also hinder the process if they are not asked to be involved.

It will be helpful to gain the support of church program staff who work in the ministry area related to the work of the nonprofit. If your nonprofit will work in the area of youth development, for example, people in the church will probably be very interested in what the youth minister or children's pastor thinks. Some members may feel a sense of loyalty to these staff members and might wonder, for example, if the feelings of the children's pastor will be hurt if the nonprofit proposes to launch a major mentoring program focused on elementary youth.

Involve key staff members early in the process, inviting them to offer their ideas about the nonprofit. They will likely bring expertise that you need and will feel that they are being included in the launching of an exciting new ministry, rather than being excluded from a splinter group that may infringe on their "turf." You could include them on a steering committee that is considering the formation of the nonprofit. Sometimes informal conversations work just as well—have lunch regularly or schedule coffee time with key staff every week or every month.

Once the nonprofit is formed, be sure to be in regular communication with these program staff members, as there is great value in coordinating the work of the nonprofit and the church if both organizations are working to serve a similar group of people. For example, members of the church youth group may be potential "customers" for a youth arts academy organized under the nonprofit. Church youth could also serve on an advisory committee that helps the nonprofit design programs. Some of the kids could even be volunteer teachers or part-time paid staff. In addition, the church program and nonprofit program could work together on fundraising and volunteer recruitment. If you coordinate your efforts, you may be able to secure more resources.

_____ We have the support of key lay leaders, at least some of whom serve on the church board.

Recruiting a group of key lay leaders to help shepherd the formation of the nonprofit is critical. They will bring excitement about the nonprofit and the new ministry into the congregation and church leadership circles. They will also bring their relationships with other church leaders as well as knowledge of how things get done within the congregation. The strong support of at least several key leaders will communicate that there is a "critical mass" of people within the church serving as "cheerleaders" for the nonprofit.

In your group of lay leaders, you may want to consider including the board chair of the church (if he or she has time), as well as other key church board members and committee chairs (personnel, trustees, and finance committees are a good bet). Involving one or more representatives from the church board on your initial planning committee may make it easier to get church board approval for the new nonprofit. Even if your church structure does not require church board approval, keeping the church board members informed is valuable.

Key leaders within the congregation, however, do not always have a formal title. Be aware of those church members who have a great deal of influence within your congregation, even if they do not hold the title of "board member." The voice of these "influencers" should be heard early on in the process.

One way to involve key lay leaders is to form an advisory or steering committee to develop a proposal about the formation of the nonprofit, or form an ad hoc group of church board members to work on the issue. If you select people based on their skills, you can bring together the talent you need for key phases of the nonprofit launch—attorneys and accountants, for example, and church members with strategic planning, public relations, and program development skills.

_____ We have some money for nonprofit start-up costs.

You do not need much money to start a nonprofit, but you do need some. At the very least, you need several hundred dollars for the filing fees to become a nonprofit (see chapter 9: Legal Issues). You may also need to pay an attorney to file the paperwork for you. If this is all the money you can raise, you may be able to secure in-kind donations for the rest.

You could, for example, ask if the church is willing to donate office space and supplies and use of a telephone and computer. A church staff member (it may be the pastor) can serve as the first executive director, overseeing the nonprofit's launch until funds can be secured to hire staff for the nonprofit. Volunteers from the church who have fundraising experience may be willing to write your first grant proposals seeking program funding. New programs operating under the nonprofit can be staffed by volunteers from the church. You may even be able to arrange for church program staff to donate some of their time to launch a program until you have raised enough money to hire program staff for the nonprofit.

The ideal scenario would be to raise money from several existing key donors for the formal launch of the nonprofit. You could seek financial support from interested people within your church or from supporters outside the church, such as other partner churches or from your denomination. It may be difficult to secure start-up funding from corporations or foundations, since they are often looking to support programs with a track record.

Ideally, you would raise enough money to cover the following costs for a period at the beginning of the life of your nonprofit (perhaps six months to a year, or longer if you can raise the money):

- the salary for an executive director (even part-time) who will handle the launch of the organization.
- staff time for fundraising. If the executive director does not possess fundraising skills, hire a consultant to prepare some initial grant proposals. The proposals should focus on the one or two programs that are key to achieving your ministry dream.
- office space.
- telephone line, computer and other office equipment.
- office supplies.
- letterhead and envelopes with the nonprofit's name printed on them.
- printing of a promotional brochure or flyer about the nonprofit.
- money for a special event launching the nonprofit, to which church and community members would be invited.
- bank fees and checks with the nonprofit's name printed on them.

What If We Are Not Ready?

What if you could only check a few items on the previous list? What if you couldn't check any? This does not mean that starting a nonprofit is completely out of the picture for your church. It may simply mean that you need to wait awhile before you begin.

Use the waiting time to build your capacity so that your church is more ready to form a nonprofit when the time is right. Gaining the support of the pastor and key staff could be a critical first step for your congregation. Or you might spend the time forming a steering committee that could develop strategies for responding to some of the other issues. That committee could develop a fundraising plan or work to define a clear mission and niche for the nonprofit.

Deciding that you are not ready at this time could simply be a pause in the process, not the end of it. One of my friends likes to describe this as the "comma" before the next part of the plot unfolds. So, even if your congregation is not ready now, you could decide to take the steps and get yourselves ready soon.

Readiness Worksheet

Check off the items that currently apply to your church congregation.

_____   We have a ministry dream that cannot be realized without the nonprofit.

_____   We want to develop a ministry that extends beyond the church congregation or the core ministry areas of the church.

_____   The ministry we are proposing is wanted and needed by the community we wish to serve.

_____   We have defined a clear niche and mission for our proposed nonprofit.

_____   The senior pastor of our church supports the development of the nonprofit.

_____   Other key church staff support the development of the nonprofit.

_____   We have the support of key lay leaders, at least some of whom serve on the church board.

_____   We have some money for nonprofit start-up costs.

4

Defining Your Mission and Niche

The Church of the Last But Not Least Apostles is located in a historic urban neighborhood that has experienced many challenges within the past decade. Eighty years ago, the neighborhood attracted some of the wealthiest families in the city who spared no expense in building large, ornate homes. Today, the community struggles with growing crime, unemployment, and a housing crisis.

The church has been at this location for nearly a hundred years and is seen by community residents as a safe place where the staff members are compassionate and helpful. It is common for neighborhood residents to come into the church during the week seeking help for a variety of family crises. The church set up a small food shelf to help with some of the basic needs, but many families also struggle with unemployment, inadequate housing, and a lack of medical care. The schools in the neighborhood are seen as some of the worst in the state, based on the low test scores received by students in both reading and math.

The church staff frequently feels overwhelmed by the number of people seeking help. Some staff members spend several hours almost every day responding to emergency requests.

After a period of low attendance in the 1970s and '80s, the Church of the Last But Not Least Apostles began to grow, and many new families have joined the church in the last five years. There is a renewed interest in community ministry among congregation members, many of whom work as counselors, social workers, and in other helping professions. It is this new interest in outreach that has sparked discussions about founding a nonprofit organization to develop new programs that address issues in the surrounding neighborhood.

A steering committee has been formed for the new nonprofit, and committee members are having a difficult time agreeing on a specific mission for the proposed organization. A number of people on the committee believe that the nonprofit should have a broad vision that encompasses as many of the neighborhood's needs as possible. They say that the organization exists to serve the community and should try to be a "one stop shop" for community residents, providing housing, food, job training, educational programs for youth, medical care, and a host of other programs. There are those on the committee, however, who believe the nonprofit should be more focused, working on needs that are not being addressed by other organizations and that match the skills and calling of the congregation.

About half of the churches I have worked with have faced a dilemma like the one described above. With so many needs and people to respond to, how can you develop an organization with a focused mission? Everyone I interviewed for this book identified mission and vision as key to the success of a church-based nonprofit. Without a sharply focused mission, nonprofits tend to "wander and struggle," as one leader put it. Another said that lacking a clear mission caused his organization to chase grant funds for a program that may not have been wise for them to undertake.

Defining your mission and niche will not be an easy process. It may take awhile. People will probably disagree with each other as you try to move forward. You may feel very tired at times as you work to make the mission sharper. But defining your mission and niche early in the process will make all of the other steps of forming your organization much easier. You will be able to develop programs, raise funds, recruit volunteers and staff, and secure partners much more effectively if others can understand clearly what it is that you have set out to do. Someone once said, "If you don't stand for something, you'll fall for anything." In defining your mission and niche, you are making sure that your nonprofit will not pursue just anything, and that it has a specific "something" that it is pursuing.

Know Your Community

Getting to know the community that your nonprofit will focus on is a critical step in defining your mission. To start, work on getting answers to several key questions: What are the primary issues in your community? How do the people in the community want the church to respond to those issues? And probably most important: Do the people in your community actually want the ministry you are proposing? Your nonprofit will be most successful if you can answer yes to this question. Like a business owner, nonprofit leaders must always be asking themselves, "Is this what our customers really want?" For example, if your nonprofit wants to provide a midnight basketball program to neighborhood youth, how do you know that is what the kids want and need?

It is pretty easy to stay within the four walls of the church and make assumptions about the lives of the people in the broader community. It is more difficult to actually build relationships with community residents and grow in your understanding of their needs and desires. It takes more time too.

There are tremendous advantages, however, to building your nonprofit's ministry on what the community says it wants. If you take the time to build these relationships, your nonprofit will focus its efforts on meeting unmet needs, rather than duplicating what other groups are already doing. You will also have a strong foundation for sustaining your programs. Strong relationships with your community will make it easier to recruit participants and volunteers and raise money.

Sunny Kang, pastor of Woodland United Methodist Church in Duluth and a Partnership Advocate for the Self Development of People Committee (PCUSA), describes a process that one of his churches used to get to know the community:

> A church I was pastor of did research for six months before we opened our doors to the community. We talked to the kids at the high school next door to the church and asked them "what is the problem in the community, what can we do to help, how can we serve you?" They were real reticent at first, but eventually they did tell us "there are a few things you could do."
>
> We ended up opening the church to kids during lunch because there were 450 students in two of the lunch periods and the school

could only accommodate 200 of them. So 200–250 kids had to leave the school building every day for lunch, even in 20 below zero weather in the winter. So we opened our building and served lunch. It started slowly at first, but grew so that we had 250–350 kids in the church building every day during the week. Too many churches say "we think the people in the community need this," and they impose their value system on the people. Community residents often end up saying to the church "Who asked you to do this?" You need to keep asking—is there a market for what we say the community might need?

So how can you get to know the community? I am not necessarily defining *community* as a geographic area, though many church-based nonprofits are focused on a neighborhood, town, or region. Your community might be a certain group of people; for example, pastors, or people living with HIV/AIDS. Here are some strategies to help you connect with the people your nonprofit aims to serve.

Connect with key leaders of the community on a one-to-one basis and build relationships with them. They will be able to introduce you to others you need to know and will help educate you on the needs and desires of the community. Start by asking them to teach you about the community. Everyone likes to share what he or she knows.

Key leaders could include:

- political leaders
- denominational staff
- pastors of other churches
- law enforcement
- staff at the neighborhood public school
- other nonprofit leaders
- program specialists in the program area that is your focus (for example, youth development, family counseling, or chemical dependency treatment)

Read the demographic data and relevant studies. Census data is valuable to ministries that are geographically based because it gives a breakdown of the area by age, race, gender, and income level. There may also be written assessments of the need you are trying to address, so you do not need to start from scratch. Public schools could have valuable demographic information on your community, as could the chamber of commerce, business associations, or neighborhood groups. Searching the Internet may help you find university research on your focus area. You might be able to find studies and statistics on infant mortality, employment and graduation rates, or housing trends that could help you focus the mission of your nonprofit.

Connect with the community through your church members. Members of your church may live in the area you aim to serve or work in professions that would provide needed contacts. If your downtown church wants to provide an outreach to the business community through the nonprofit, for example, business leaders in your church could help you accomplish your goal.

Join community organizations or boards. If a group of people from the community is working on an issue you would like to address, consider joining the group. As you work side by side, you will hear community concerns articulated over and over again. You will also build new relationships with community leaders; for example, a crime task force for the neighborhood or town you hope to serve would be a great place to connect. Always ask: "What can the church do to support the community?"

Attend community meetings. When community members get together for discussions or celebrations, make sure there is at least one member of your church in attendance. You may want to consider building a portable booth for community events to promote the visibility of the congregation and the nonprofit.

Walk around the community. There is no substitute for just walking around the community to see the people and the needs with your own eyes. If you are open to spontaneous conversations, you will learn a great deal from people you meet on the street. Find out where people just "hang out" in your community—it could be the neighborhood park or the diner in your rural town. If your community is not geographically based, just plan on attending whenever the people of your "community" get together. It might be a national conference on a particular topic or a denominational gathering.

Gather the opinions of the community. If the people you want to serve have a positive impression of the church, they may be willing to participate in a survey or focus group. Invite some folks over for dinner at the church and ask them what they think. Brief door-to-door surveys might also do the trick. Try to find a volunteer who has the expertise to help you develop a survey; for example, there may be someone in your congregation who has worked with focus groups. Also, your local neighborhood organization or United Way might be able to advise you on how to design a questionnaire. Questions for surveys or focus groups should focus around the questions: What do you see as the major issues for this community? How would you like to see this church respond to those issues? How can the church serve you?

Every Need Is Not A Call

Occasionally people (usually funders) complain to me about ministry organizations. They usually say something like this: "That group is so unfocused. They try to respond to every need they see! I'm waiting for them to pick just one or two areas to work on. Then I'll be interested."

I cannot disagree, because my work with ministry organizations has shown me that many do indeed lack focus. "What's your mission?" is a simple question, but many ministry groups respond to it with a complex laundry list of programs and community needs: "We want to help people in our neighborhood with everything they need: food, clothing, medical care, housing, job training, and child care. Oh, and there will be programs for men and a private K–12 school too." Generally speaking, a more focused vision and mission leads to greater success.

In response to these "laundry list" mission statements, one of my friends with 26 years of ministry experience likes to say, "Remember, every need is not a call." That is, just because we see an unmet need does not mean that our congregation should leap into action to try to meet it. At the very least, trying to address every need we see stretches churches so thin that it makes it more difficult to provide high quality ministries. When we try to meet every need, we often end up not meeting any.

As people of faith, many of us are filled with compassion when we see anyone who needs help. Our hearts go out to people who are struggling and we want to do something to help them right now. The impulse behind this is pure, but I have watched it lead to more ill conceived and poorly implemented programs than I can count. If a church forges ahead without considering whether it has the capacity to deliver the proposed ministry, it may very well fail. There are many other issues to consider as well; for example, whether there are other organizations working on this issue or problem, or whether the church has a particular call from God for this ministry.

A Sharply Focused Mission

So how can you get to the place where your nonprofit has a sharply focused mission? You will need to articulate the following:

Who is your ministry for? Describe in as much detail as you can the people or institutions that your organization will work with and for. Some organizations define this more broadly, such as "all residents of the North Side neighborhood." Other groups are very specific, focusing on "youth between the ages of eight and 12" or "teenage parents," for example. The "who" in your mission could be focused on institutions instead of groups of people. In this case, your mission might state "all of the churches in our denomination," or "public schools in Lake County."

Where are you going to do it? Will you work in your neighborhood, your town, your region or nationally? You will need to decide whether there are geographic boundaries to the work of your nonprofit. Many churches develop a nonprofit to launch community ministry in the geographic area around their church. It may help others to understand your mission statement if you choose a geographic area that is generally recognizable; for example, "the Phillips neighborhood," or the "South Side," or the "Tri-state area."

What are you going to do? Describe in general terms what your organization is trying to do. Are you helping people learn how to read? Providing health care? Or maybe your work is to train pastors to develop effective outreach programs. Your mission statement may also include a few words on how you expect the people of your community to be impacted by your efforts—"becoming economically self-sufficient," "graduating from high school," or "living in safe, affordable housing."

How are you going to do it? The "how" provides some qualifiers about what you are trying to do. Part of this is identifying your values as an organization. For example, your mission statement might say that you will do your work "in collaboration," "based on the teachings of Jesus Christ," or "with the strong input of your community."

Ascertaining the Call

Most churches have at least one ministry they are "called" to; that is, the church is not just responding to a need or doing something because it ought to. Instead, there is a deep and abiding sense within the congregation and the staff that this is the right thing for the church to do at this time.

I wanted to highlight this notion because finding a calling is different than having a good idea or becoming aware of a need. Some churches I have worked with operate as though any good idea brought forward by a member should be acted upon, and I strongly disagree with that practice. If we all marched forward whenever anyone said, "Go!" who knows where we would end up?

Finding the calling is similar to discovering your "ministry dream," though your dream will probably be more about a specific program. A calling is a sense of being drawn toward a certain aspect of God's work in the world; for example, evangelism or acts of mercy toward the poor.

Faith traditions and denominations differ concerning the meaning of a call and how it will be revealed. As explained in chapter 2 on the ministry dream, some congregations focus more on the pastor's vision, while others expect ministry to "bubble up" from lay leaders. In one church I worked with, the choir director was a real visionary and would say things during his introduction to Sunday morning worship that inspired the congregation to move forward into new ministry.

God will often choose to reveal the call through the special gifts and characteristics of your congregation. You may receive God's direction through prayer or teaching or worship or whatever it is that makes up the "flavor" of your church. If your church has a high regard for prophetic gifts, for example, watch the people with those gifts to see if they have a sense of the calling.

You may suspect that your church is hearing a new call if one or more of the following things begin to happen:

- People in your congregation start praying about a particular need or situation.
- The teachers and preachers in your congregation begin to speak about particular Scriptures concerning the situation.
- People with prophetic gifts (prophecy, visions, discernment) begin to talk about God's desire for the church to move in this ministry direction.
- A small group of congregation members feel a passion for something and begin to discuss what the church could do in this new ministry area. Some of them may sacrifice their time or financial resources to begin ministry on a small scale, such as a "pilot program."
- One or more staff members feel a burning desire to move forward in a new ministry direction, and they start encouraging the church to consider it.
- The capacity to lead in this new ministry area becomes apparent within the church. People with the necessary program skills step forward, for example, or the church becomes aware of a way that interested congregation members could be trained to fulfill this new call.
- The resources for the ministry (people, money, space, etc.) arrive just at the moment they are needed.

While I worked at Park Avenue, I knew God was pushing us toward new ministry when different people kept approaching me with the same ministry idea. When you tune in to the unique ways that God is calling the people of your church, you will begin to envision a whole new landscape of ministry.

Finding Your Niche and Collaborating with Others

Understanding how your nonprofit fits with work already being done by other groups is also an important part of defining your organization. One of the questions funders like to ask is: "How is your program related to the work of other, similar organizations working in your area?" It is a great question. Finding the answer to this question can help you:

- focus the work of your nonprofit on the areas of greatest unmet need
- help you avoid duplicating the work of other organizations
- help you identify organizations you could partner with in your work

A wonderful resource for you to use in understanding how to work within your community is *Building Communities from the Inside Out*, a book by John L. McKnight and John P. Kretzmann (ACTA, 1993). This book describes how to implement "asset-based community development"; that is, focusing on the assets and skills possessed by community residents and institutions, not their deficits and needs. The book includes an excellent chapter on how local religious institutions can be involved in community renewal, citing creative examples from all around the country.

Finding Your Niche

Your niche is the unique work of your nonprofit. Maybe you serve a group of people that no one else does. You might work in a geographical area that is served by few other groups. Perhaps it is that your program focus is unique or innovative. Maybe it is the way that you implement it; for example, the faith focus or level of intensity. Understanding your niche will help you focus your efforts and will also aid in fundraising and recruiting volunteers. People get excited about work that is new and innovative and that meets real needs.

To find your niche, you will need to gain a good understanding of what other similar groups are doing. If you are a geographically based group, try driving around your area to see where other similar organizations are located. Arrange to visit them during program hours and talk with program staff about the work of the organization. Some cities and towns have indexes of groups doing human service work (try your United Way) and you can find organizations that way as well. Avoid limiting your search to other nonprofits or churches. Public schools, governmental agencies, or businesses might be working in your program focus area as well.

From my experience, good old-fashioned networking is one of the best ways to connect with other organizations. Start with someone you know who works in the field and connect with the people they suggest. Then ask that person whom you should talk with. You will end up with a "chain" of connected people who will help educate you about the work being done in your nonprofit's focus area.

As you connect with other groups look for similarities with your nonprofit in:

- the type of program being offered
- the type of people served by other organizations
- the geographic focus
- other church-based programs

Opportunities for Collaboration

If you do find other groups that are doing similar work in your community, it is not necessarily a bad sign. You may be able to collaborate with one or more of them and make a greater impact as a result.

Collaboration does not seem to be a top priority for many faith-based groups, and this is unfortunate. From my experience, many church-based ministries seem reticent to work with other groups in the community, particularly secular ones, perhaps because they are afraid that these other groups will somehow "contaminate" the mission of the church. Many ministries also fall prey to the idea that they need to be "one stop shops" that provide all of the services that a particular individual or family needs. This idea keeps the focus on what one nonprofit can and should be doing, rather than on ways the community can work together to address its own issues.

If you do it right, collaboration could bring many new resources into your ministry. It can also add expertise and community connections that will be critical to your success.

Your collaborations will be most successful if you look for groups that are a good fit with yours. Look for a similar mission and values, as well as staff members who have the potential to work well together. Collaborations that fail usually fall apart over style differences, not substance. That is, you may be pursuing the same mission as a partner organization, but you are both going about it in such a different way that it becomes impossible to work together.

The following are some ideas for working together with other organizations in your community:

- Share space. Many churches around the country lease or donate some of the space in their facility to community groups.
- Share staff. If each organization can only afford to hire one outreach worker at 20 hours a week, for example, you might be able to hire the same person and share them. Sharing administrative staff and consultants may also be more efficient than trying to hire them on your own.
- Purchase equipment and supplies together in order to get a better price.
- Share expertise.
- Fundraise together. "Collaborate, collaborate" is now a favorite tune of many funders. Submitting a grant application together may very well improve your chances of getting the money.
- Share community connections. A partner group may have ties to public officials, neighborhood leaders, or other nonprofit directors who you need to know.

Making an Impact
without
Starting a New Program or Organization

Your church may be able to have a significant impact on community issues without starting a new program or organization yourselves. Sometimes the greatest contribution a church can make is to the work of others. This can be hard to swallow, since we all like to feel that a program is "ours" alone. You may decide that your church just does not have the capacity to meet particular community needs, or that the congregation does not feel a strong enough "call" for you to start your own organization or program. There may be other groups working on the issue, however, that would welcome your support!

There are many wonderful ways that your church can make a contribution without starting your own program or nonprofit:

- Send church volunteers out to give their time.
- Contribute some church staff time to a community project.
- Send money!
- Make in-kind contributions of supplies, food, vehicle use, and so forth.
- Let other groups use the church building as a gathering place for meetings, rallies, and celebrations.
- Join a formal collaboration of other organizations.
- Advocate for public policy changes. Encourage your congregation to stay informed on public policy issues and to vote their consciences.
- Lend the church's name as a sponsor for community events or meetings.

An interesting example of churches providing support without starting their own program is KidsCare, a program of TURN (Twin Cities Urban Reconciliation Network) in Minneapolis and St. Paul. Child care providers are required by Minnesota law to have about $200 of equipment (including a fire extinguisher and a portable crib) in order to be licensed, and this expense was keeping some people from going into the business. KidsCare recruits churches to provide start-up equipment for home-based child care. Churches that lacked the capacity to open their own day care center helped increase the number of day care slots by supporting in-home providers through the program.

Putting Legs on Your Dream

Taking a big dream and molding it into a mission can be exhausting work. In my experience, the dream stage is more fun, because working on the mission brings home the stark reality of just how much work needs to be done. But try to think of it this way: developing the mission gives "legs" to your dream, helping people outside of your congregation understand what it is you are trying to do. This helps your dream take flight, as more people understand it and become committed to making it a reality.

Identifying the Mission and Niche of Your Nonprofit

Key Questions

What other groups are doing similar work in our area?

What makes the work of our nonprofit unique by comparison?

How can we connect with other organizations doing similar work?

I.   Community Needs and Wants
     What does our community tell us about their needs and wants?

     How we have connected with the community we wish to serve?

II. The Mission of the Nonprofit
     What is the mission of our nonprofit?

Whom will we serve?

Where will we do it?

What will we do?

How will we do it?

The Call of the Church

Does your congregation have a call to do the work described in the mission of the nonprofit?

If yes, in what specific ways is God revealing the call?

Describe the ministry that your congregation is called to:

Control versus Autonomy:
How Much Control Will the Church Have Over the Nonprofit?

Hands and Feet Temple wants to open a day care center and has decided to start up a separate nonprofit to house the new program. The day care idea took shape quickly and now the church is working hard to get the new nonprofit up and running. A report issued by the state identified the three-square-mile area around the church as having fewer day care slots and a higher need for them than any other area in the state. In response to the report, the state legislature set aside special funding for the neediest areas, and Hands and Feet has been asked to apply for some of this grant money.

Hands and Feet Day Care (the name of the new nonprofit) has been recognized by the state as a nonprofit, and paperwork to obtain tax exemption is pending with the Internal Revenue Service. The church board has been governing the new nonprofit since it was officially organized two months ago, and now a separate board has been formed that includes some church members, parents from the community, day care experts, local politicians, and clergy of other churches.

The new board dives right in and makes the following decisions:

- *authorizes the nonprofit's executive director to sign a contract with the state, accepting the grant money to develop the new day care center*
- *approves the hiring of five new staff people to develop programming for the center and conduct community outreach*
- *has preliminary discussions with a local construction company concerning the development of a new facility for the day care*

When leaders at the church hear about the actions of the new board, many of them are offended that they were not kept in the loop.

They wonder if the new board actually has the authority to make these decisions and if the church will have any control over or input into the day care, a ministry that many people in the church feel passionate about. The nonprofit's leaders believe that they are "just doing their jobs"—moving ahead with the development of the new day care center as opportunities for funding, staffing, and a new facility present themselves.

"Who's in control?" has been a key question for just about every church I have ever worked with. Control can be a difficult thing to discuss for those with a more egalitarian view of the world, but the bottom line is this: it is important to decide who has the authority to make decisions within an organization. This is often more complicated than finding out who the senior pastor or chair of the board is. As I have described in previous chapters, sometimes church members without a big title are just as powerful as those in appointed positions.

Spending time discussing the issue of control at the outset will save you a lot of conflict and misunderstanding later; for example, if the nonprofit expects to be able to hire its own staff but the church board expects to approve the hiring decisions, you have a problem. All sorts of misunderstandings can arise if you do not discuss the issue of control from the very beginning.

Control and autonomy are ends of a continuum. Your congregation may choose to be closer to one of the ends, giving the church substantial authority to oversee the nonprofit. Or maybe you will choose to be near the other end, where the nonprofit is given the authority to oversee itself. Just keep in mind that there is a lot of room in the middle to work out an approach that gives both organizations some authority to manage the nonprofit.

The following kinds of questions may arise early in the life of the nonprofit, and it will be helpful to locate where you are on the control versus autonomy continuum with each:

Who approves the strategic plan for the nonprofit?
a. the church board and key church staff
b. the nonprofit board and key nonprofit staff
c. both a and b
d. an ad hoc committee composed of church members and nonprofit staff and board members

If the nonprofit wants to change its mission statement or add a major new program, does the church get a say in it?
a.   Yes; the pastor and church board must approve these changes.
b.   Yes; the congregation as a whole provides input and the nonprofit board makes the final decisions.
c.   No; these decisions are made by nonprofit staff and board members.

Who has the authority to hire program staff for the nonprofit?
a.   the pastor of the church
b.   the church board
c.   the church's personnel committee
d.   the executive director of the nonprofit
e.   nonprofit board
f.   a hiring committee composed of key church leaders and members of the nonprofit's board

Who needs to approve the nonprofit's annual budget?
a.   the finance committee of the church
b.   the church board
c.   the nonprofit board
d.   all of the above

Are the nonprofit's staff accountable to the church board?
a.   Yes; the nonprofit staff is hired by the church board.
b.   Yes; the nonprofit staff, though supervised by the executive director of the nonprofit, is required to make quarterly reports of activity to the church board.
c.   No; the nonprofit staff is accountable to the nonprofit board.

Weighing the Benefits and Risks of Control and Autonomy

There are both benefits and risks to giving the church significant control over the nonprofit; there are also benefits and risks to giving the nonprofit a great deal of autonomy. It is important as you discuss control and autonomy that you weigh the benefits and risks of each. Depending on the culture and theology of your church, you may see one of these concepts as the "enemy." Instead, try to consider these ideas as neutral, each with its own benefits and challenges.

Benefits and Risks of Control

The primary benefit of greater control by the church is that the nonprofit stays closely linked to the mission and people of the church. When your church board and lay leaders help shape and govern the nonprofit, there is a greater likelihood that the nonprofit will stay in alignment with the church's mission and vision. This can be a wonderful outcome, as the two organizations work together toward the same end.

Tying the nonprofit more closely to the church also gives a larger group of people a sense of ownership for the nonprofit. With more workers from the congregation sharing their skills, time, and financial resources, you may very well end up with a better product in the end.

The downside of greater control is that it can stifle new ministry ideas that may need a more free and flexible environment to flourish. If the church places too many restrictions on the nonprofit, a significant portion of the new organization's resources could be focused on reporting to the church instead of "hatching" the new ministry. It could also be very discouraging for the staff and board members of the nonprofit if they perceive that accountability required by the church indicates mistrust. Also, the more people, committees, and institutions involved, the more time it takes (sometimes a lot more time) to move forward.

Benefits and Risks of Autonomy

The main benefit to greater autonomy is that the new nonprofit has the freedom necessary to launch new ministry ideas. The new group will not be constrained by the procedures, politics, or personalities of the church. The staff and volunteers you need for the beginning stages of your organization may prefer to work in an environment with more autonomy, without a lot of restrictions imposed by the church. These "ministry entrepreneurs" are much needed as you develop the organization and its programs from scratch. They will come and stay if you let them truly exercise their gifts of big-picture visioning and development.

The primary challenge of greater autonomy is that the nonprofit could more easily drift apart from the church in both its mission and in the way it operates. For example, it may be easier for the nonprofit at your church to drift away from its faith roots if it is not tied into the church in both its policies and structure. Other examples of conflicts between churches and nonprofits (arising in part from a structure with high autonomy for the nonprofit) include disagreements over how much input community residents should have, whether or not to work with churches of other denominations, and whether buying up property is a community development strategy that fits with the mission of the church.

Another challenge is that the people of the church could more easily lose a sense of ownership for the ministry of the nonprofit. Then the nonprofit loses out on all of those skills, funds, and volunteer hours within the congregation that were described previously.

A Mixture of the Two

Your church may decide on a hybrid of the two approaches: greater control in some areas and more autonomy in others. Usually, I see churches choose the hybrid approach when trust has been violated around a certain issue and the church wants to retain a degree of control until trust is rebuilt.

Your church may want to require high accountability around financial issues only: bookkeeping practices and good stewardship of the funds that are received. This may be the right choice because of a recent breach of trust within the church; for example, funds being mismanaged or poorly spent. Perhaps your congregation is particularly sensitive about personnel decisions because a church staff member has recently been terminated for poor performance. It was so painful for everyone that church members want to ensure that everything is done just right the next time.

When Control Is Useful

There are several areas where the church may want to exercise control over the nonprofit. My bias is against micromanagement of the nonprofit by church leaders, so my list below focuses on big-picture issues.

Certainly, one option is for you to set things up so that the nonprofit operates almost totally independently of the church, without formal accountability in any of the areas described below. Use the following list as a basis for a discussion about how the church expects to stay involved once the nonprofit is launched.

Check off areas where you think the church needs to exercise control. There is space for you to list your own ideas about how this could happen.

Mission and Strategic Direction

The church may decide it would like to be involved in designing or approving any changes in the "big picture" of the nonprofit.

_____ changes in the mission or vision statement
_____ developing a new strategic plan
_____ adding a program focus area
_____ changing the geographic area served
_____ changing the population served (for example, expanding a youth service program to include families)
_____ other

Scandals or Legal Troubles

Some churches decide to intervene in the management of the nonprofit only if there is trouble; for example, if a legal claim is filed against the nonprofit or if there is evidence that the organization and its finances are being mismanaged.

_____ serious concerns about management of the nonprofit's finances
_____ sexual harassment or sexual abuse claims
_____ serious injury of program participants, staff or volunteers
_____ a lawsuit filed against the nonprofit
_____ negative media publicity
_____ other

Financial Management

The church may want to exercise some oversight in financial management to ensure that the nonprofit is managing resources adequately. Connecting regularly with the finance committee of the church could be one way to accomplish this.

____ approval of annual budget of the nonprofit and any major changes in it during the course of the year

____ approval of the annual audit of the nonprofit

____ periodic review of the nonprofit's financial statements throughout the year (for example, monthly or quarterly)

____ involvement if there are shortfalls or deficits

____ approval of changes in financial procedures (check signers, money counting, and so forth)

____ approval of any major investments made by the nonprofit

____ other

Fundraising Goals or Plans

The church may want to approve the amount that the nonprofit proposes to raise as well as the plan that describes potential sources of funding.

____ approval of annual fundraising goal and plan

____ approval of capital campaign goals and plans

____ approval of budget for any fundraising activity with significant up-front costs (for example, a fundraising event or telemarketing campaign)

Selection and Nomination of Board Members for the Nonprofit

The nominating committee for the church may want to be involved in this in some way, especially if the nonprofit will be recruiting church members to serve on its board.

____ oversight of the nomination process

____ final approval of the slate of recommended board members

Hiring or Firing of Staff

The personnel committee of the church or the church board may want to be involved in these issues. Possible involvement by the church could include:

_____ approval of any new positions within the nonprofit
_____ approval of job descriptions and hiring processes
_____ approval of salary ranges and personnel policies
_____ giving the final "thumbs up" to recommended candidates
_____ involvement in disputes or disagreements between nonprofit staff and the executive director of the nonprofit or the nonprofit's board of directors
_____ vote on termination of staff
_____ other

Creation of New Programs

The church may want to ensure that any new programs launched under the nonprofit fit with the church's mission.

_____ approval of new program ideas
_____ church representation on the committee that designs the new program
_____ final approval of program plan
_____ regular reports on program progress and outcomes
_____ other

Facility Purchase or Renovation

The congregation, church board, or trustees may want to approve the steps toward building purchase or renovation. Some denominations mandate a particular process around the purchase of property—several congregational votes, for example, or approval by the local or regional office of the denomination.

_____ approval of proposal to purchase property
_____ approval of proposal to build facilities
_____ approval of proposal to renovate or expand existing facilities
_____ other

Entering into Major Contracts or Collaborations with New Partners

The church may want to give final approval to any major new contracts or collaborations that the nonprofit will engage in. At the very least, church leaders will want to be kept informed about the following:

____   entering into contractual obligations with new partners
____   approving major new collaborative relationships with new partners
____   other

Other Key Issues to Consider

So far, we have looked at the impact of church control on the nonprofit's function and its ability to achieve its mission. You should also consider the following issues as you make decisions about church control and the autonomy of the nonprofit.

Trusting Each Other

Regardless of whether you choose a great deal of control, total autonomy, or something in between, there will need to be a significant level of trust between the church and the nonprofit in order for this relationship to succeed. When a church sets up a nonprofit, it is, at the very least, letting go of some of the details of the ministry that will be under the nonprofit's umbrella. The nonprofit is a brand-new separate entity, and the new staff, board, and volunteers within it need to be empowered to move forward with the ministry dream. If church staff and members are always questioning decisions made by the nonprofit's leaders, the atmosphere of mistrust that is created will impede the progress of the nonprofit.

We are called as people of faith to find ways to build trusting, positive relationships with each other. Keep this reality in front of you as you proceed with the discussion of control and autonomy, as it can easily spiral down into a consideration of the "worst case scenarios" or "people behaving as badly as we can imagine." Make sure that you are also spending time and energy on the "best case scenarios," imagining what could happen if everyone involved rises to the occasion and acts with integrity.

Rules of Your Denomination

Before you make decisions on these issues, make sure you are aware of your denomination's rules about how much control the church retains over the nonprofit. Some denominations have formal documents that describe how the church is to remain connected with "affiliate organizations" or "connected nonprofits." These documents may spell out expectations about how the church board is to remain involved or what the role of the pastor should be with the nonprofit. The role of church committees may also be described. One of the denominations I have worked with requires the church personnel committee to make all hiring decisions related to the nonprofit. So check out the Methodist Discipline, the Presbyterian Book of Order, or your particular denomination's document before you proceed any further.

Theological Considerations

In some congregations, the issue of control versus autonomy is a theological one. Congregations with more of a focus on control and accountability frequently emphasize the authoritative role of the pastor to cast vision and oversee all ministries of the church. Lay people and church staff members have a high accountability to the people at the "top" of the organization.

In this setting, you would expect to find a nonprofit that is very interconnected with the church, with the pastor and church board members playing key roles in overseeing the ministry of the nonprofit. The pastor may serve as president or board chair of the nonprofit, and may supervise at least some of the nonprofit's staff. The church board would probably have some oversight of the nonprofit, signing off on key decisions such as the hiring of staff and the approval of the annual budget.

Other congregations prefer to use an "equipping and sending" model that gives lay members a great deal of autonomy to dream and develop ministries. At a church using this model, you would expect to find a nonprofit that operates with its own, independent board of directors and staff. The church would help recruit board members and program volunteers with the needed skills, then "send" them out as ministers to the nonprofit. The nonprofit board and staff would have the authority to make decisions about hiring, budgets, program development, and strategic planning and would not be required to get approval from the church on these and other key issues.

Avoid Micromanagement by the Church

When I am describing "control," I do not mean that the church should get involved in managing the minute details of the nonprofit. From my experience, it just is not productive for a large group of people to make decisions about which curriculum to purchase, how many brochures to print, or whether to serve donuts or cookies at an event. I am advocating big-picture accountability—letting others do the preliminary work and signing off on the final decision.

I have been at plenty of church meetings where the discussion focused on the tiny details, which ended up being unproductive for everybody involved. One reason this occurs is that many church boards and committees are composed of people who are representing a particular ministry area. These folks are good at dealing with the details—many of them were selected because they can manage the "small picture" well. When pulled together into a group discussion, they simply talk about what they know.

Micromanagement by the church can hinder the ministries of the nonprofit and frustrate its staff and volunteers. It communicates mistrust—an unwillingness to let the people of the nonprofit manage the everyday details of their organization.

Whoever leads the discussion about launching the nonprofit needs to be keenly aware of this issue, always guiding the process to focus on big-picture accountability. If you can establish a "norm" early on of letting the staff and volunteers of the nonprofit manage the day-to-day affairs of the organization, you will get much farther and faster.

Key Questions

Are there particular areas where your church would want to exercise more control over the nonprofit? List them.

Are there certain areas in which the nonprofit will have more autonomy? List them.

What are the rules of your denomination regarding the control the church exercises over an affiliated nonprofit?

Does your church have key theological beliefs that will influence whether you choose greater control by the church or greater autonomy for the nonprofit?

6

The Role of the Board of Directors

It is a conversation that I have about once a week, on average. An executive director of a nonprofit will call and say: "I'm just so frustrated with my board right now. We're at a critical point for the organization—we have so many opportunities for new programs and partnerships if we could just raise the funds. But all the board wants to do is get involved in the minute details of running the organization. I need them to let go of supervising staff, running programs, and staffing the office. What I really need is a committed group that will promote our organization and get out there and ask for money."

Much of the frustration and tension described above can be avoided if your nonprofit decides two things early on:

1. The type of board you need. Do you need a tactical one that will run the organization? Or a navigational one that will manage the big picture only?
2. The specific duties of your board members. Write a job description before you begin recruiting the board, and there will be much less confusion about who is supposed to be doing what.

Let Your Ministry Dream Drive the Decisions

As I advocated in a previous chapter, it is important to stay focused on your ministry dream as you make decisions about the nonprofit's board of directors. Discussions about authority and decision making in a church setting can quickly become less about the ministry and more about who is in control.

Instead, try to keep the spotlight focused on who and what you need to move the ministry forward.

Boards can be a blessing and they can be a curse. A lot will depend on how well you define the role of your board. Set a tone early on that the board "really does not need to do much," and you will get your wish—a group of people who might show up to meetings but do little else. Define your board as a group that is fully engaged with the organization, bringing expertise and resources into the ministry, and your board members may become so valuable to the organization that you may wonder how you ever lived without them.

The Fiduciary Duties of the Board of Directors

The board of a legally incorporated nonprofit organization is both financially and legally responsible for the organization. The law calls this these "fiduciary duties" of a nonprofit board, which is the nonnegotiable part of serving on a board of directors. Members of a board have these duties whether they like it or not. This may be a new concept for your church, since many church boards focus more on managing programs and less on financial and legal oversight.

The attorney you work with or your state's office of the attorney general or secretary of state can provide you with information on your state's specific laws regarding board member fiduciary duties. Generally, these duties can be summarized as follows:

The Duty of Care

Board members have the responsibility to take good care of the organization. This includes attending meetings and ensuring that the resources of the organization are used wisely. In addition, board members are responsible for ensuring that accurate records are kept and that any reports of theft or mismanagement are investigated.

The Duty of Loyalty

Board members must have an undivided loyalty to the organization, always putting the good of the organization first. Board members must not use the organization to financially benefit themselves or their family members; for example, board members should not divert corporate business opportunities for personal gain.

The Duty of Obedience

Members of the board must obey the law in overseeing the affairs of the organization. This includes the rules that the organization has established for itself in its bylaws and articles of incorporation as well as state and federal statutes.

Different Types of Boards

All boards must fulfill the fiduciary duties described in the previous section; however, they do have the flexibility to define how they want to go about doing the work of the nonprofit. From my experience, there are basically two kinds of boards—the hands-on or "tactical" board, and the big-picture or "navigational" board. Once you identify the type of board you need, you will also need to decide how you expect board members to get involved with fundraising.

Much has been written about what nonprofit boards do, what they should and should not be, and how you can get them to do what you want. Reading some of this material (see materials about boards listed in the bibliography) will help you as you work on forming the board for your nonprofit.

The Tactical Board

The tactical board is the type many organizations start out with. Under the tactical model, board members are much more directly involved in the day-to-day operations of the organization. The nonprofit probably has few paid staff at this point, and has not hired an executive director yet. The board meets frequently (monthly or more often) and you will likely find board members engaged in the following types of hands-on tasks:

- developing programs (developing plans, recruiting volunteers and staff, and securing supplies among many other tasks)
- writing grants, proposals, and newsletters
- "running" the office (answering the phone and correspondence about the organization, other clerical tasks)
- overseeing community relations (attending community meetings and serving on boards, task forces)

The tactical board works well when an organization is in its infancy, because board members can provide the energy needed to "jump-start" the organization into existence. The disadvantage of this model is that board members are volunteers, and tasks may not get completed quickly if members do not have sufficient time to devote to them.

The Navigational Board

The navigational board oversees the big picture for the nonprofit but has very limited involvement in the day-to-day operations of the organization. Typically, paid staff has the responsibility for implementing programs, running the office, preparing written materials such as grants and newsletters, and connecting with community organizations.

The navigational board may meet less often than a tactical board (monthly, quarterly, or less often) and may break itself down into committees that focus on particular task areas such as strategic planning, resource development, and personnel. On this type of board, you will frequently find members engaged in the following types of navigational tasks:

- developing and reviewing the strategic plan for the organization
- evaluating the performance of the executive director
- reviewing and approving the annual budget and audit
- ensuring that the organization meets its annual goals for programs and operations

The navigational board works well when there are paid staff to run the daily operations of the nonprofit. In fact, it almost becomes necessary to shift to this board model when an organization grows larger and more complex, since board members may not have the time or expertise to actually "run" the organization as they would under the tactical model.

A Job Description for Board Members

Having a written job description for the board of directors helps everyone understand what the board's job is. Staff members know what they can expect of the board, and board members are clear from the outset what it is that they are supposed to be doing. Having the job description will help in recruiting new board members, as new recruits typically ask, "What will I be expected to do?"

If you are forming a first-time board for the nonprofit, the steering committee that is making plans for the new organization should develop the job description. Then the board and key staff should review it periodically (probably annually) to decide if it still meets the needs of the nonprofit. The job description can also help the board evaluate its own performance. The question can be asked annually: "Are we fulfilling our responsibilities as a board?"

A job description appropriate for a navigational board of directors might include the following kinds of duties:

Spiritual Leadership. Perform duties in manner that is consistent with the spiritual principles of the organization (or, for example, "scriptural principles" or "the teachings of Jesus Christ"), particularly _____ (beliefs could be articulated here).

Strategic Planning. Oversee strategic planning efforts for the nonprofit; review strategic plan annually to check the organization's progress against the goals.

Evaluation. Ensure that all programs and staff are evaluated at least annually. Review evaluation reports to identify areas for improvement and oversee development of plan to address these issues.

Financial Oversight. Approve annual budget and any significant changes made to the budget during the year. Monitor cash flow, and ensure that an audit of the organization's finances is conducted annually.

Legal Issues. Ensure that organization is in compliance with all relevant laws and regulations. Ensure that there are adequate risk management procedures, including the purchase of necessary liability insurance.

Personnel Issues. Hire, supervise, and evaluate the executive director; develop and approve personnel policies for the organization.

Communications/Promotions. Ensure that the organization has a communications plan. Promote the organization whenever possible through business and personal contacts.

Resource Development. Ensure that the organization has adequate resources for its programs and operations. (If you want your board to be directly involved in fundraising, add language such as: "Raise funds for the organization from foundation, corporate, and individual sources. Plan and implement special fundraising events.")

Fundraising by Board Members

"Will board members be expected to raise money?" is a difficult question for many nonprofits to address, so if it seems difficult to talk about, that's because it is! Your board members may come to the nonprofit with little fundraising experience, and they may be uncomfortable getting involved in this aspect of your organization, at least at first. This does not mean, however, that you cannot successfully involve your board members in fundraising—it is possible for them to be trained and mobilized to do this much-needed work.

There are varying opinions in the nonprofit sector about whether board members need to be engaged in fundraising for the nonprofit or not. It is important to communicate to board members from the very beginning, during the recruitment process if possible, whether fundraising will be a part of their duties. Honest communication will help you build strong relationships with your board members from the start.

I have made the mistake myself of "surprising" board members with this responsibility, thinking that they might not agree to serve on the board if they knew that fundraising was a part of the deal. I can tell you that this strategy does not work!

One view of board fundraising is that the board must be significantly engaged in fundraising for the nonprofit; in fact, some nonprofit leaders say that fundraising is the most important board responsibility. People in this camp might say: "Your board members are some of the closest people to your organization. They should care enough about it to ask their colleagues and friends to support it. Their willingness to fundraise will demonstrate to the community that this is an organization worth supporting." When fundraising is the major emphasis for a board, members are typically chosen (at least in part) for their connections and personal wealth. Some organizations bring board members on with the understanding that they will give at a certain level and raise a certain amount of money—usually several thousand dollars at the very least.

Another view of board membership focuses less on fundraising and more on the ability of board members to govern the organization and lend their expertise to it. Board members are chosen for their planning and management expertise. You would recruit people who can help the organization navigate the big picture as it moves into the future. Program expertise and insight is also important under this model. A day care center might choose one or more day care providers to serve on its board; a youth development nonprofit might invite youth specialists from other agencies to serve. Community participation is also key under this view of the board— inviting people onto the board from your "customer" base will give key stakeholders a voice into how the mission of the organization is shaped.

Creative Ways to Engage Your Board
in Fundraising

Even if you decide that fundraising will be a major board responsibility, chances are good that you will have to select at least some people for your board who are not wealthy people with lots of fundraising contacts. Most church-based nonprofits end up choosing a diversity of board members in order to stay connected to key stakeholders—the church and the community in particular.

I hope you will decide to recruit at least some board members who can help you with fundraising. You may want to look for someone in your congregation or community with a high-level position at a local company—a board member like this can help draw in significant corporate grants. Another type of board member to look for is one who is part of a "giving culture" with their friends and colleagues, all of whom are people of means who give generously to each other's charities.

Even if only some of your board members are wealthy or well connected, all board members can participate in fundraising in some way. Here are some suggestions for engaging your board members in the fundraising process.

Ask all board members to make financial gifts to the organization each year. This is critical to being able to raise foundation money, since outside funders want to see that the people closest to the organization support it financially. If your board is not willing to support the organization, why should they?

The best approach is to have the board chair send a letter and make an announcement at a board meeting about the importance of giving. The chair should follow up individually with board members if necessary.

Set a positive tone when asking board members to give. Communicate to them that you are asking them to make a gift that is significant for them—whether it is $10 or $10,000. Make sure they know that all gifts are needed and welcome, and that board members are not valued based on the amount of money they give.

Recruit board members from partner churches. If there are churches you are targeting for financial support of your nonprofit, invite an active member or leader from that church to serve on your board. In recent years, church giving to missions and community projects has become more tied to member involvement.

Ask board members to approach their employer for a gift. Foundations and corporations love to give to organizations where their employees are involved, and board membership is viewed by many as the highest level of involvement.

Check out board member connections with community-based funding or government grants. Some of your board members may participate in block clubs or neighborhood associations that may have access to special "pots" of money. Perhaps your nonprofit could be part of a neighborhood, citywide, or regional coalition that applies for funds. Some board members may also work in government and may be able to provide advice on how to access funding within their department.

See if board members can secure in-kind gifts for the nonprofit. You might be surprised what they will find. Past boards I have worked with have secured office furniture, food, books, computers, and software.

Ask board members to organize a fundraising event and invite their friends and colleagues. Some folks feel uncomfortable asking their friends for an outright gift to a charity, but they would not hesitate to invite them to a golf tournament, a concert, or a dinner or auction. Fundraising events work best if there is an enthusiastic group of board members (and maybe other volunteers as well) who "own" the event, planning and organizing it and assuming responsibility for getting people to attend it.

What Makes a Faith-Based Board Different?

All nonprofit boards are called to operate with integrity and high ethical standards. This call is even deeper for faith-based nonprofits, because of the spiritual and theological beliefs on which they are founded. Beliefs about good stewardship of resources, reconciliation between all people, and respect for human life could influence decisions made by the boards of faith-based organizations. Many faith-based groups also feel a call to a public witness, which would be hindered by scandal or ethical breaches.

It is not unusual for faith-based boards to pursue decision making differently than the boards of secular organizations. Depending on the traditions in your church, prayer, Bible study, and fasting may precede significant decisions made by the board of your nonprofit. You may even want to set aside time for these spiritual discernment activities at board meetings.

James B. Lemler, dean and president of Seabury-Western Theological Seminary in Evanston, Illinois, and an ordained priest in the Episcopal Church, describes the rich faith traditions that can lead faith-based boards in their decision making in *Serving Those in Need*, edited by Edward L. Queen II:

> Board members in faith-based organizations are called to be aware of the theological foundations that enable and empower their service and their leadership. Rich resources of prayer, spirituality, Scripture, and tradition undergird their work. . . . If faith-based service organizations are distinctive from secular ones, it must be that the spirit of God enriches their work and their deliberations. The tradition of so many faiths in viewing decision making as a spiritual and prayerful process needs to be reinvigorated and revived (San Francisco: Jossey-Bass, 2000, p. 74).

The role of the faith-based board is not only to adhere to the theological beliefs set before it, but also to serve as an example to others about how faith can be lived out in the world. Your nonprofit board may live out their faith in new ways, challenging the people of the church and community to greater action and a new level of commitment.

Talking to each other about the theological beliefs and ethical standards that undergird your work can help you to better understand them and to "hold tight" to them in a crisis. You may even want to write them down, including them as part of your strategic plan in the "Values of the Organization" section or as part of your board's job description. Some of your beliefs might include:

- good stewardship of resources
- caring for the poor and needy
- giving 10 percent of income (the biblical concept of tithing)
- not charging interest on loans made to individuals or organizations
- developing inclusive leadership that involves women and people of many cultural groups
- equipping the "saints" for ministry
- refusing funding from organizations that promote activities considered destructive to the community, including smoking, gambling, and alcohol.

Getting the Board You Want

Making decisions early on about the role of the board and choosing your board members carefully can help your new nonprofit move forward in ways you could not have imagined. Board members can add so much when they clearly understand the mission of the organization and how they can best work to achieve it. In my own experience, board members have brought encouragement, expertise, money, wisdom, community connections, and a whole host of other assets. These assets were most likely to be present when I followed the advice I have given in this chapter. Spend time defining roles and choose your board members carefully.

Key Questions

Defining the Role of the Board

What do we need the board of our nonprofit to do in order to move the nonprofit and its ministries forward?

Do we need a tactical or navigational board? Why?

How do we want the board to be involved in fundraising?

What are the key spiritual beliefs and practices that we want the nonprofit board to live out?

Write out a job description for your nonprofit's board.

7

Structuring Your Board of Directors

Now that you have identified what you expect the nonprofit's board members to do, you can decide on a board structure that will help your nonprofit move forward. Again, it is important for you to be motivated by what moves the ministry dream forward, rather than by what is easiest or least controversial.

I have identified three models in this chapter, and you may discover additional ones as you talk with your steering committee and the church board.

Model 1: The Church Board Also Serves as the Nonprofit's Board
Model 2: A Separate Board for the Nonprofit Has Accountability to the Church
Model 3: A Completely Separate Board Oversees the Nonprofit

My Experience

When I first began work as the executive director of the Park Avenue Foundation, the organization was governed by the administrative board of the church. It was a challenge for the church board to devote much time to the foundation, because the church was dealing with so much pressing business at the time. I remember one particularly frustrating church board meeting when I presented the new strategic plan for the Park Avenue Foundation—the discussion took only about five minutes.

Another frustrating development was that some corporate and foundation funders had reduced or cut their contributions to the foundation because we did not have representatives from their organizations on our board. The church board was composed of committee chairs or at-large members elected by the congregation, so the foundation was unable to choose board members based on their ability to help with fundraising.

So I suggested that we form a separate board for the Park Avenue Foundation. For some reason, I expected everyone to embrace the idea from the outset, since I thought it was so clear that the foundation needed people to govern it who had the time, connections, and specific expertise the organization needed. To move on to the next level of ministry, we really needed a new group of people, empowered to do the specific work of the Park Avenue Foundation.

That, of course, is not what happened. Forming a separate board for the Park Avenue Foundation was not an idea that was immediately embraced by the church. Instead, it was a controversial proposal that required a great deal of preparation before it passed the church board about six months later. A number of church leaders were afraid to let the foundation have any measure of independence from the church. Most of their fear was related to the departure of the foundation's founder, who had left the organization about 18 months earlier and ended up starting a congregation and affiliated nonprofit in the same neighborhood. Some church members and financial supporters had followed him.

In meetings about the proposed separate board, we spent a great deal of time imagining the worst-case scenarios. Would the nonprofit start to do things that violated the mission of the church? Could the executive director (me) have free reign without any accountability to church leaders? What if the foundation board made a decision that made the church look bad or was inconsistent with the church's mission? One elderly member of the board kept reminding people about a church down the street that had started a nonprofit in the 1960s. The nonprofit had completely separated from the church and become a huge organization without a faith focus. Would that happen to us as well?

I must confess it was exhausting to spend this much time focusing on what could go wrong, but I think people needed to do it to feel confident that we had built a model that was right for that particular time at Park Avenue. We ended up using model 2, in which the nonprofit had its own board, but with accountability to the church board and pastoral staff. Written right into the nonprofit's bylaws were the foundation's connections with the church and its leaders:

- The staff and parish relations committee of the church were given authority to handle all personnel matters. The committee was given authority to hire, fire, and create personnel policies for the nonprofit's staff.
- The finance committee of the church was responsible for keeping an eye on foundation finances. They reviewed foundation financial reports at least quarterly and reviewed the budget and audit of the foundation before the foundation board approved them.
- The trustees of the church were responsible for overseeing the care of all property owned by the nonprofit.
- The administrative board of the church reserved the right to provide direction to the nonprofit to ensure that actions taken by the nonprofit were consistent with the mission of the church.
- The senior pastor served as president of the foundation and supervised the executive director and program staff.

A Word about Advisory Boards

When I refer to "the board" in this chapter, I am referring to the governing board of the church or nonprofit, as opposed to an advisory board. The difference between these two types of boards is important for you to understand. The governing board of an organization is the group of people that has accepted legal and financial responsibility for it. This type of board fulfills the fiduciary duties described in the previous chapter. There is no higher authority within the organization than the governing board.

An advisory board is very different from a governing board in that it exists only to advise the organization about specific issues. It is not a decision-making or policy-making body. Advisory boards are often formed around specific issues or projects and are composed of people with expertise in that area. In addition to having a governing board, for example, you may want to form an advisory board on youth issues in the community that includes youth and parents as well as staff members from organizations that serve youth.

My only caution about having both a governing board and advisory board is that the people on the advisory board may get confused about how much authority they actually have. If they are connected to a specific program, for example, they might get the idea that they are the ones who are responsible for hiring and firing staff. If that is not true, it can be very frustrating for them and could put you in a difficult position with potential staff members. So be sure to communicate carefully with board members about their duties. Preparing a job description (described in the previous chapter) will help eliminate some possible confusion about the role of board members.

Four Preliminary Steps

Your decisions about how to structure your board should be based on what you know about the four key issues that we reviewed in chapter 5: Control versus Autonomy (see pp.54-64). Here we will dig deeper into these four issues, which are:

1.   level of trust
2.   management areas where the church will want more control
3.   type of board members you will need
4.   denominational rules that will affect your board model

   Identify the level of trust within your church now. The board model you choose will, in part, depend on how much your church members trust each other. If there has recently been a split in your church or a difficult event that has caused church members to mistrust each other and the church leadership, then there might be reluctance to spin off a nonprofit that operates independently of the congregation. Some congregations are continuously factionalized, breaking into distinct groups that argue about each issue that arises within the church. A board model with closer ties to the church might be the right choice if you are in either of these situations.

   Identify management areas where the church will want more control or oversight. As you consider the board models, you might recognize a desire for the church to maintain more control or accountability only in certain areas. That is, the nonprofit would be fairly independent of the church, with its own board, but would be accountable to the church around personnel issues, financial management, or facilities. If there has been a recent problem or a breach of trust in one particular area, the church may want to maintain more control in that one area until the nonprofit is more established and is better able to assume responsibility.

Identify the types of board members you will need in order to move the organization and its ministries forward. What are the skills and connections you need board members to bring to the organization in order to move it forward? Take a look at the board job description you have developed and see what types of skills you are looking for in board members. If the skills you need can only be found outside of your church, you will want to choose either model 2 or model 3, both of which allow the nonprofit to form its own board with at least some members who are not a part of the congregation.

Identify any denominational requirements that will influence your nonprofit's board structure. Make sure you understand what your denomination requires concerning your nonprofit's board structure. Some denominations require that the church board and committees have at least some oversight of the nonprofit; others leave it entirely up to each congregation to decide how to structure the new organization.

Key Questions

Preliminary Steps to Deciding on a Board Structure

On a scale of 1 to 10, how much do people in your church trust each other? (1 = very low trust, 10 = very high trust)

Are there management areas of the nonprofit where the church would want more control or oversight? If so, list them. (Examples include financial management, personnel, building management.)

What type of people will you need on the board to move the organization forward? (Refer to your board member job description.)

Are there any denominational requirements that will influence your choice of a board structure? List them.

Description of the Three Board Models

Model 1:
The Church Board Also Serves as the Nonprofit's Board

You might not realize that the governing board of your church can also serve as the nonprofit's board (see figure 1 on the following page). You can even hold the meeting about nonprofit business on the same night as the church board meeting (though I would not recommend it if your church board meetings are lengthy to begin with).

One of the chief advantages to this model is that it allows the nonprofit to get started on its work without investing the time it takes to form a brand new board. So if there is a sense of urgency within the congregation about moving forward with the ministry dream, you may want to start with this model.

Another advantage to this model is that it helps keeps the church and nonprofit closely tied together, making it easier to stay in sync in mission and purpose. It also helps to ensure that the people of the church will continue to feel a sense of ownership for the nonprofit. It is difficult for church members to say, "That's the work that's going on over there," when church leaders are so involved in governing the new organization.

This model may be a good fit if your congregation is structured around a centralized authority, focusing on the important role of the pastor and key staff and lay leaders in moving new ministries forward. In a congregation that is organized in this way, new ministry ideas tend to come from the pastor or staff in key positions. Lay leaders at the top of the organization may also play an important role. Church members expect the people in these positions to be responsible for the leadership of the organization and its ministries.

The key disadvantage to this model is that it limits the nonprofit from expanding beyond the church's policies, politics, and people. Your church processes may be too slow and labyrinthine for a nonprofit ministry that requires quick action.

In addition, there is much less flexibility in the selection of board members for the nonprofit under this model. Churches typically have a well-articulated process for how their own board members are selected. The nonprofit will have to live within this and "take whoever they get" on the board. This could be a severe limitation for the nonprofit if board members with particular skills and connections are needed. Also, depending on how pressing church business is, your church board may simply not have the necessary time to devote to the nonprofit.

One way to draw in needed expertise under this model is to form an advisory board composed of people who can provide advice on management or program areas of the nonprofit. Also, advisory board members may have more time than the church board to work out some of the details of the nonprofit's programs. Keep in mind, however, that an advisory board does not make decisions on behalf of the nonprofit; it can only provide advice. The church board is still the governing board of the nonprofit and is in the decision-making role.

Figure 1

Model 1:
The Church Board Also Serves as the Nonprofit's Board

Elements of this model:
- church board convenes separately as the nonprofit board, possibly on the same night that the church board meets
- advisory committee to the church board could be formed, with people who have more expertise in certain areas and more time to devote to advising the nonprofit

Table 7.1

Model 1:
The Church Board Also Serves as the Nonprofit's Board

Pros of This Model	Cons of This Model
• Strong connection to the church and its leadership	• Less control over who serves on the board
• Can begin work with the nonprofit quickly, do not have to wait to form a board	• Church and nonprofit may need different kinds of board members due to: — different purpose for organization — different pace of work — different skills needed — different networks needed
• May be a good way to start: build trust with the nonprofit first, form separate board later	• Church board could have little time to devote to the nonprofit, if there is pressing church business

Works well for churches with:
- a brand new nonprofit
- a strong or recent history of division or disunity
- a "strong leader" or "centralized authority" theology
- enough time at church board meetings to properly address the nonprofit

Would be a challenge for churches with:
- an "equipping and sending" theology, decentralized structure
- a ministry vision that requires participation from people outside the church
- a ministry vision that needs to proceed with a pace or culture different from the church's

Model 2:
A Separate Board for the Nonprofit That Has Accountability to the Church

In model 2 (see figure 2 on page 91), the nonprofit develops its own board, which has at least some accountability to the church and its leaders. This is a hybrid of the other two models, giving the nonprofit more independence than model 1 but also providing for stronger ties to the church and its ministries than model 3.

Developing this model will require more thought and planning than the other two, since you will have to make decisions about several areas of oversight that the church could have. The model is flexible, allowing you to choose the areas where the church would like to have more accountability from the nonprofit. You could choose, for example, for the church board to approve the nonprofit's budget and strategic plan every year but leave hiring decisions entirely in the hands of the nonprofit's board.

One of the strengths of this model is that the nonprofit can intentionally select at least some of its own board members from outside of the church. Being able to recruit board members based on their skills and connections may enable you to bring someone onto the board who works for a major local corporation. This could help you secure grants from the company's foundation.

I should add, however, that it can be difficult to have a board composed of people from both inside and outside of the church. Board members that you bring in from the outside may possess values and theologies different from those of the people in the church. They may also differ in their views of the community and in their expectations about the pace at which the board will act.

One of the key differences I have found on boards is between business leaders and church leaders. Business leaders are used to working quickly; some of them work in companies where people respond immediately when they snap their fingers. When these business leaders come up against the relative slow pace of church life and the lengthy processes frequently used by community-based organizations, they may feel frustrated. They may also try to remold the nonprofit in the corporate image. Having a diversity of people and viewpoints on your board can be a real blessing, giving you the benefit of many voices as the nonprofit is formed. You need to be prepared, however, to mediate some of the conflicts that may arise because of the diversity.

Another bonus of model 2 is that it can create a natural way for the church and nonprofit to stay connected and communicating. If you choose the option of having church staff or members serve on the nonprofit board, you will not have to work quite as hard at keeping the church in the loop.

As issues are raised at nonprofit board meetings, you may find that church members will say things like: "The church is planning something similar later this year. Could we work together?" or "I wonder if the church would let us use its equipment for that program?" Under this model, you could have church members right in your board meetings who have the connections that will help the nonprofit secure what it needs from the church; for example, additional resources, facilities, people, and the good will of other church leaders. So keeping the church and its leaders in the loop through board membership can open up many opportunities for collaboration and partnership. It will also help you avoid misunderstanding and conflict.

One of the challenges of this model is that it is more difficult to administrate and manage than the other two. This is mostly because the roles of the nonprofit and the church are not as clear. Both organizations still own the work of the nonprofit and are sharing power in the management of the new organization. This more complex structure means that more time and energy needs to be spent on communicating who has the authority to do what and fulfilling reporting duties.

If, for instance, you opt to have the church board sign off on some of the decisions made by the nonprofit board, someone has to move the decision through the process once the nonprofit board has approved it. Someone must get the issue on the church board agenda, send out information to church board members, show up at their meeting to make a report, and then report to the nonprofit board about what happened. We used this model at Park Avenue, and I often felt like I was playing tennis with all of the running back and forth between the two governing boards. If your church has limited administrative capacity or if you are having difficulty managing just one board of directors, then this might not be the model for you.

Another challenge of this model is that it does not allow the nonprofit as much freedom and flexibility as model 3. Under model 2, the nonprofit will have to include some board members from the church, or submit some of its management decisions to church leaders, or both.

How to Implement This Model

There are a number of options for you to consider as you implement model 2. Basically, you are revisiting the issue of how much control or accountability the church expects from the nonprofit. Under model 2, you can opt for a tight connection to the church or a fairly loose one. Accountability to the church can come in three forms: through board member selection, through church oversight of certain management areas of the nonprofit, and through supervision of nonprofit staff by church staff (usually the pastor). You may decide to include one, two, or all three of these options in your model.

A Direct Connection to the Church through Board Membership

Placing certain types of people on the nonprofit's board could help the church maintain a strong connection to the nonprofit. Having one or more of the pastors serve on the nonprofit board would be one way to accomplish this, or you could invite other key staff or lay leaders to serve.

Some church-based nonprofits require that a certain percentage (often the majority) of the nonprofit's board members also be church members. This leaves room to invite board members from the community but keeps the interests of the church at the forefront. You may also want to designate one shared board member who would serve on both the church board and the nonprofit board.

Church Oversight of Management Areas of the Nonprofit

Another option is for the church to require more accountability from the nonprofit in certain management areas. This was described in detail in chapter 5: Control versus Autonomy (pp. 54-64). The church could choose to be more involved in some aspects of the nonprofit and less involved in others.

First you need to identify the type of decisions the church would like to have oversight of. Does the church want to review all decisions made by the nonprofit board? I hope not, as this would be micromanagement of the new organization and would hinder it in its ability to move forward with the ministry dream. As I mentioned in a previous chapter, boards need to focus on big-picture decisions made by the nonprofit instead of the small details. Types of decisions made by the nonprofit that could be reviewed by the church include:

- major policy decisions such as the annual budget, strategic plan, and approval of a new program initiative.
- big-picture or vision issues. The church has input into any changes in the mission and vision of the nonprofit
- any decisions affecting the alignment of the church and the nonprofit.

For example, if the church is committed to serving its immediate neighborhood and the nonprofit decides to expand beyond that geographic area, church leaders may ask to be involved in making this decision.

Review the list on pages 59-62 with your steering committee and key church leaders to choose the management areas for the closest church oversight. Briefly, the management areas are:

- mission and strategic direction
- legal issues or scandals
- selection and nomination of board members for the nonprofit
- human resources
- creation of new programs
- financial management
- facility purchase or renovation
- entering into major contracts or collaborations with new partners

Figure 2

Model 2:
A Separate Board for the Nonprofit
That Has Accountability to the Church

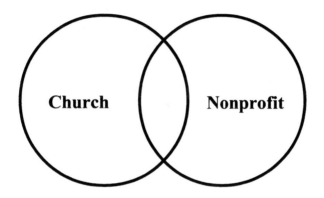

Elements of This Model

A separate board for the nonprofit is formed, but its structure intentionally ties it to the church:

- some nonprofit board members come from outside the church and one or more of the following options:
- some members of the church board also serve on the nonprofit board
- a certain percentage of the nonprofit's board are required to be members of the church
- the church board has the authority to approve or overturn decisions made by the nonprofit board

It is important to identify which kinds of decisions can be approved or overturned:

Table 7.2

Model 2:
A Separate Board for the Nonprofit
That Has Accountability to the Church

All decisions	Big-picture or vision issues
Ethical/legal problems	Alignment issues—the nonprofit becomes "out of sync" with the church
Major policy decisions; i.e., annual budget/audit, strategic plan	

Table 7.3

Model 2:
A Separate Board for the Nonprofit
That Has Accountability to the Church

Pros of This Model	Cons of This Model
• Creates the opportunity for the church and nonprofit to be in alignment with each other	• Can be a challenge to bring together people from inside and outside the church on the board
• Creates natural communication channels between church and nonprofit	— differences in values — differences in theology — differences in how they view the community — differences in work culture/ pace of work
• Can intentionally select nonprofit board members with the right mix of: — expertise — community connection — networks and partners — fundraising contacts	• A more complicated structure to administrate
• Congregation still feels a sense of ownership for the ministries of the nonprofit	— more reporting requirements — recruiting board members is more complicated

Works well for churches with:
• a ministry vision that requires people from outside the church
• and an openness to involving them
• some history of conflict and division

Would be a challenge for churches with:
• poor administrative capacity
• limited trust in people from outside the church

Model 3:
A Completely Separate Board Oversees the Nonprofit

In this model, the nonprofit has its own board of directors, but it has no formal accountabilities to the church. For example, the nonprofit is not required to have church members on its board, nor is it required to submit decisions to church review.

Of the three board models described, model 3 provides the greatest autonomy and flexibility for the nonprofit. Board members for the nonprofit are selected based on their expertise, networks, and values, rather than their ties to the church. So if you decided that you needed four corporate executives, four housing specialists, and four community residents on your board, you could go out and get them.

This model works well for ministries that need to operate very differently from the church. If you are pursuing a ministry dream that requires quick action, this model might be the one for you. Model 3 may also fit your church if you operate with an "equipping and sending" theology in ministry. If your standard way of doing business is to encourage church members to develop ministry ideas and then pursue them with little interference from or accountability to the church, you could encourage the development of the nonprofit in the same way using this board structure.

With this model, there is always the danger that the nonprofit will become disconnected from the people and the mission of the church. Without any requirement to have board members or approval from the church, it will be more difficult for the two organizations to stay connected. Everyone involved with the nonprofit might agree that communicating with the church is critical, but it may end up being the last task on the list once the nonprofit is launched and consumed by operating its ministries. Without an interlocked structure to keep you together, it will be more difficult to stay in touch and move in the same direction.

In some extreme cases I am aware of, a structure like this has created disunity and conflict, causing the people involved to choose "camps," some siding with the nonprofit and its leaders, others siding with the church and the pastor. This model does not necessarily have to lead you there, but you will have to work harder to avoid it. Also, people who are determined to promote division and conflict will usually find a way to do it regardless of the structure of the organization.

Figure 3

Model 3:
A Completely Separate Board Oversees the Nonprofit

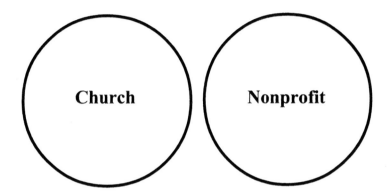

Elements of This Model

- A separate board is formed for the nonprofit without structural ties to the church.
- Board members for the nonprofit are selected on the basis of their expertise, connections, and values, rather than their ties to the church.
- Communication between the church board and the nonprofit board becomes even more essential, since it will not be accomplished through structural ties between the two organizations.

Table 7.3

Model 3:
A Completely Separate Board for the Nonprofit

Pros of This Model	Cons of This Model
• Complete freedom to recruit the board members that the nonprofit needs	• Harder to stay connected to the church's mission and its leadership
• Freedom for the nonprofit to establish its own culture and work at its own pace	• Could lead to disunity/split between the church and the nonprofit

Works well for churches with:
- a high trust level
- an "equipping and sending" theology
- a vision for ministry that would require the nonprofit to work differently from the church

Would be a challenge for churches with:
- a lack of trust
- a poor ability to communicate
- no administrative capacity

Choosing a Model That Works for You

There really is no one best board model. The one you choose will depend a great deal on the values you hold as an organization, the type of board members you will need, and the requirements of your denomination. Whether your congregation likes "top-down" or "bottom-up" decision-making processes will also play a role, as will the history and culture of your church.

As you work through the process of choosing your board model, I hope you will review all three options. You may be surprised by the model that seems to suit your organization best once you have taken a close look at all three models. Plus, the model that you aspire to implement someday may not be where you start. For example, I have worked with a number of congregations that chose model 1 (the church board also serves as the nonprofit's board) to begin but worked toward having a separate board for the nonprofit within a year or two of the organization's founding.

Key Questions

Revisit your answers to Key Questions: Preliminary Steps on page 83.

Based on the answers to these four preliminary questions, which board model are you pointed towards?

Using a highlighter pen, review the pros and cons list for each of the three board models, highlighting each of the pluses and challenges that seem to describe your situation best.

You may want to complete this exercise as a group if you are working with a steering committee, a subgroup of your church board, or key staff and lay leaders.

Model 1: The Church Board Also Serves as the Nonprofit's Board
Number of pluses_____   Number of challenges_____

Model 2: A Separate Board for the Nonprofit Has Accountability to the Church
Number of pluses_____   Number of challenges_____

Model 3: A Completely Separate Board Oversees the Nonprofit
Number of pluses_____   Number of challenges_____

8

Personnel Issues

"You have to help me figure out this staffing issue," a local pastor said to me one day. "We found a person right in our own congregation who we thought would make a perfect executive director for our nonprofit. He had worked for community organizations before, and even though he didn't have a lot of experience with supervision, fundraising, or program development, he seemed eager to learn. So we hired him six months ago, but it just isn't working out. This staff person is great at running programs, but doesn't know anything about running an organization or leading an entire staff. We didn't realize the difference, because we really didn't develop a specific job description before we hired him. The hard thing is that the person has a lot of friends and family members in the church. How can I let him go without causing a huge conflict within our congregation?"

When it comes to personnel matters, you can plan to avoid problems like the one described above, or you can plan to spend months (even years) recovering from personnel mistakes. This topic covers a lot of ground and, unfortunately, I cannot cover all aspects of it in this chapter. I have tried to identify, however, the personnel issues that are unique to a church-based nonprofit. Be sure to discuss these issues in the early planning stages of your organization so that you are able to choose the most qualified staff members possible. A strong staff that is hired at the outset can move your organization farther than you ever imagined. A weak or ineffective staff will hinder your progress and sap the energy of the organization.

Any new organization needs to put the following in place, to insure that quality personnel are selected and retained. There are many resources on the following topics that will help you set up this area of your nonprofit; two are listed in the bibliography of this book. You will need to develop:

- job descriptions
- a strategy to recruit candidates for the open position(s)
- interviewing strategies and processes
- personnel policies
- salary ranges and a benefits plan

Personnel Policies and Salary Ranges

Before you hire staff for the nonprofit, you will need to decide if the nonprofit will create its own set of personnel policies and salary ranges or abide by the church's policies in these areas. Sorting this out early on can help you avoid confusion and conflict later. It can also help you attract high-quality staff to the nonprofit—a key ingredient for ministry success.

If the idea of developing salary ranges and personnel policies is a new one for your church, let me offer a few reasons about why having these in place is so important. Having salary ranges and policies will communicate to potential staff that your organization does its homework, takes itself seriously, and takes employees seriously. This may allow you to attract higher quality candidates with a greater level of experience.

A set of personnel policies will also give your group the framework to treat all candidates and employees the same when it comes to hiring, firing, and grievance procedures. For example, if one day care teacher is dismissed for poor performance after only three months and another day care teacher who is also performing poorly is allowed to stay, employees and community members (perhaps the congregation too) may perceive that there has been unjust or unequal treatment of staff. This can seriously damage employee morale and may land your organization in court as well. Treating people in similar situations differently can give ammunition to a disgruntled employee who wants to prove that you discriminated against them based on age, race, or gender. If you develop salary ranges and personnel policies and follow them, they can help you avoid unjust treatment of staff and arbitrary personnel decisions.

Elements of a Personnel Policy Manual

There are many fine resources available to help you create a personnel manual for your nonprofit, and I will not attempt to re-create all of that information here. One helpful resource I have found is *The Alban Personnel Handbook for Congregations* by Edwin Berry (Alban, 1999), which provides excellent personnel policy templates and a boilerplate employee handbook.

Another great resource for you would be professionals in your congregation who work in human resources or personnel. You may even want to recruit one or more to serve on the nonprofit's board. In my experience, human resource professionals can provide invaluable advice on employee searches, interviewing processes, and resolving grievances or performance issues with employees. Professionals with experience in the nonprofit world will be the most helpful to you.

Briefly, these are the types of issues you should address in your personnel policies. Your attorney or human resources professional can help you tailor the materials to your particular needs:

- information on the different types of employees within the organization; for example, full-time, part-time, exempt, and non-exempt
- hiring processes—who interviews, who hires, employee application forms, and standardized interview questions
- pay schedules and salary ranges
- performance evaluations—how and when they will be conducted; you may also want to include the criteria for evaluation and what evaluation results will be tied to (for example, wages or job advancement)
- terms for employee termination—how and how many times employees will be notified about performance or discipline issues before termination; also, reasons for termination without notice
- sexual harassment policy—detailing how the organization will respond when sexual harassment is reported
- details on the benefits provided to employees including vacation, sick days, holidays, health and dental insurance, FICA, retirement benefits, and unpaid leave

Separate Policies and Salary Ranges for the Nonprofit

There are some good reasons to consider developing a separate set of policies and salary ranges for the nonprofit. Outside funders of the nonprofit programs, particularly government agencies, may require that certain policies be in place before funds are released to your group. For example, one church-based nonprofit I worked with contracted with state government to provide a block nurse program, providing at-home nursing care to elderly residents in the neighborhood around the church. Because funding was coming from the state, the nonprofit was required to develop a base salary for the nurses that was consistent with the requirements in state law. Funders may also require you to have an affirmative action policy to be used in the hiring of staff and vendors.

In addition, the nonprofit may need to attract different kinds of staff members than would typically work at a church. Depending on the programs developed under the nonprofit, you may need housing and economic development specialists, social workers, chemical dependency counselors, or medical personnel. If the people with these skills are in demand, the nonprofit will need to pay "the going rate" to attract and keep them, even if it means paying them more than the church staff. Also, if you do not have the right candidates for a job within your own church, you may need to remove or minimize job qualifications that require church membership or adherence to a specific theology in order to attract qualified candidates.

A good example of the possible need for separate salary ranges is the creation of an executive director position for your nonprofit. This is a position that requires a broad set of skills and experiences, and to attract a high quality candidate, you may need to pay him or her more than church program staff—you might even need to pay the executive director more than the pastor of the church. Staff members with fundraising skills, for example, a potential development director or fundraising consultant, will also likely command higher salaries. In larger organizations, it is not unusual for the top fundraiser to make more money than the president or executive director does.

A survey of local nonprofit salaries could be a useful tool as you are developing personnel policies for the new nonprofit. There may be an organization in your area that conducts these surveys and publishes a report on a regular basis. Reviewing this report can help you get your salaries "in the ballpark" once you learn what other nonprofit staff are being paid. Check with your local United Way or with the nonprofit management program at your local college or university (often these programs are part of the business school). There may also be an association for nonprofits in your state—in Minnesota it is called the Minnesota Council of Nonprofits (MCN). MCN conducts and publishes a salary survey of typical nonprofit staff positions in Minnesota on a periodic basis.

The disadvantage of having separate policies is that it can create division and mistrust between church and nonprofit staff members. If it is perceived that the nonprofit staff are valued more than church staff, or that nonprofit staff are the political favorites with the pastor and lay leaders, church staff may feel that there has been injustice in the way employees are treated. If you decide to have different salary ranges and policies for the nonprofit staff, there are a couple of ways to minimize the frustration that church staff might feel:

- If the organizations are operated separately from each other, staff members of both the church and nonprofit may see the organizations as being distinct from each other. If the nonprofit has its own board for example, and an executive director that supervises the nonprofit's staff, church staff may be less likely to see their work as being the same as or closely related to the work of the nonprofit staff.
- If the nonprofit develops staff positions that have different titles and responsibilities than the church staff, a more persuasive case can be made for having different salary ranges and policies for the nonprofit. For example, if both the church and the nonprofit need to hire youth workers with similar types of responsibilities, it will be difficult to make the case that they should be paid vastly different salaries. However, if the nonprofit needs to hire medical personnel or a fundraising director, positions unlikely to be found on the staff of a church, the nonprofit will have more freedom to develop its own policies and salaries for staff.

Types of People for the Nonprofit Staff

The Executive Director

Nonprofit organizations generally have someone who serves as the CEO; usually that position is called executive director. If there is more than one top management employee within the organization (usually only in larger nonprofits), the person in this position might also be called president. This person oversees all aspects of the nonprofit including planning, financial management, staff supervision, and resource development. They report to the board of the nonprofit and represent the organization in the community.

In the early stages of your nonprofit, someone on the church staff may temporarily serve as the executive director until you have the funds to hire someone who can dedicate all of their time to the job. I would recommend that you eventually look for someone with experience managing a nonprofit— you will need to add this expertise to your staff at some point in order to move the nonprofit forward.

Depending on what your organization needs at the time, it would be helpful for your executive director candidate to have experience in fundraising, staff supervision, strategic planning, financial management, program development, and community relations. A job description for an executive director might include the following kinds of duties:

Executive Director of XYZ Nonprofit
Reports to: Board of Directors
- Oversee all fundraising activities for the nonprofit.
- Manage strategic planning efforts for the nonprofit. Work with the board, officers, staff, and volunteers of the nonprofit to identify future directions for the organization and to develop strategic goals.
- Manage the nonprofit's finances, including developing the annual budget, and monitoring compliance with expense budgets by operations and program staff.
- Oversee communication efforts, including development of a newsletter, brochures, and other communication tools.
- Supervise all program and operations staff of the nonprofit.
- Oversee and coordinate evaluation of the programs under the nonprofit's umbrella.
- Provide leadership in program development efforts.
- Serve as a liaison to community organizations and residents.

The President

Your group may choose to have a member of the church staff or a key lay leader of the church serve as president of the nonprofit. In the context of your new nonprofit, I am suggesting that the president's position be part-time with no salary paid by the nonprofit. One of the key roles of this type of president is to serve as a liaison between the church and the nonprofit.

When you have a president in addition to an executive director, the president is not very involved in the day-to-day operations of the nonprofit, since it is the executive director's role to oversee and implement fundraising, supervise program staff, and see to it that the programs are implemented. Instead, the president's role is much more focused on the big picture—helping shape the vision and mission of the nonprofit, maintaining the relationship between the church and the nonprofit, and participating in meetings with funders and major partners.

In my experience, it is usually the senior pastor of the church who serves in this role. Depending on how your congregation is organized, however, it may be more appropriate for an associate pastor or key program staff member, such as the community ministries director or education director, to serve in this role. Also, if your congregation has appointed or elected lay leaders who have significant organizational responsibility for the church, one of them may be appropriate for the president's role. For example, some churches have a lay leader who serves as "moderator" for the entire congregation. He or she might make a great nonprofit president.

Because the president oversees the big picture of the organization (see job description below) I would recommend that you choose someone who has experience managing an entire organization, not just one or two programs. Although I suggested above that a key program staff member might be appropriate for the president's role, keep in mind that such a person may not be accustomed to thinking about the larger vision and mission of the whole organization, since managing programs can be so all-consuming.

Job Description for President of XYZ Nonprofit
Overall responsibility: To keep the vision and mission of the nonprofit and the church in alignment.
- Serve as a member of the nonprofit board of directors.
- Supervise the executive director. (You may choose to have the executive

director report to the board instead. You could also choose to have the pastor supervise the nonprofit's program staff.)

- Work with the executive director to provide leadership in strategic planning and visioning for the nonprofit.
- Mediate conflicts between the church and the nonprofit (though if your pastor is not viewed as a "neutral" party by either the church or the nonprofit, this would be more difficult for him or her to accomplish).
- Actively participate in nonprofit fundraising and promotional activities.
- Help define and implement solutions in crisis situations.
- Oversee the search for a new executive director when needed.

Fundraising Staff

Once your nonprofit reaches a certain size, it will be wise for you to consider hiring fundraising staff. If you are not ready for a full-time development director yet, hiring a fundraising consultant to get things started is a good option. A consultant could work a few hours each week or put in concentrated effort at times of the year when the nonprofit does most of its fundraising. Maybe you just need someone to prepare some boilerplate grant proposals and your volunteers can make the contacts and personalize the packages. As in most professions, some fundraising consultants are excellent and others will take your money and provide you with nothing. As you search for a consultant, look for:

- A positive recommendation from someone you know. There is no substitute for a personal recommendation.
- A proven track record of success in fundraising. Get references and call them.
- Expertise in the type of fundraising you need help with. Just know that fundraising is a broad field, and if you would like to secure government grants for your ministry, look for a consultant with specific experience in that. Someone who plans fundraising dinners probably will not be able to help you tap into state and federal funding for your programs.

Once you do get to the point of hiring a development director, do some research in your local area to see what development professionals are typically paid and develop a salary range based on that information.

As mentioned in a previous paragraph, you may have to pay an experienced development professional more than anyone else on the church or nonprofit staff, simply because their skills are in demand and it takes many years of experience to develop a track record in fundraising.

One reason to move toward adding fundraising staff is to develop a broad range of funding sources. It is common for new organizations to be dependent on just a couple of grants or on one type of funding. Adding an experienced development professional to the nonprofit staff will increase your chances of attracting funds from a wide range of sources—foundations, corporations, government, individuals, fundraising events, and earned income projects are some of the options. Having someone who works on fundraising every day for you will increase the amount of money you raise. Fundraising is a volume business—the more you ask, the more you raise. Your ideal candidate for the job would have experience in:

- grant writing, including a strong knowledge of local foundations and corporations
- securing gifts from individual donors
- planning and implementing fundraising events
- fundraising from churches and other religious organizations
- developing a planned giving program (an added plus)
- designing and implementing direct mail campaigns (an added plus)

The Role of the Pastor

The Pastor as Executive Director of the Nonprofit

Some church-based nonprofits designate the pastor as the executive director of the nonprofit. Depending on the rules of your denomination, it may even be required that the pastor serve in this role. He or she then becomes the person responsible for overseeing the organization and managing its day-to-day operations. While you may need to start your organization this way, I cannot recommend it as a long-term solution, and there are many reasons why.

The main reason for finding someone other than your pastor to serve as executive director is that most pastors simply do not have the time to add management of a separate nonprofit to their already busy schedules. This is particularly true for pastors of small churches. The pastor is preaching, teaching, visiting the sick, supervising church staff, planning meetings, recruiting volunteers, and the list goes on and on. Most nonprofits need someone who can devote a significant amount of time to it right from the outset. Also, as one of my pastor friends who was also an executive director pointed out: "Sometimes it's just more fun to work on my nonprofit tasks, so I think my work with the church suffers."

Another reason to select another person as executive director is that many pastors are not equipped with the skills needed to manage a separate nonprofit (there are exceptions, of course, like my friend with a master of divinity *and* a master of business administration in nonprofit management). While your pastor may be someone people regard as a good leader, he or she may not know much about setting up bookkeeping systems, writing grants, developing strategic plans, or writing personnel policies. Your nonprofit may eventually need an executive director who has experience in all of these things and more.

Mary Nelson, president of Bethel New Life, Inc., a nonprofit founded out of Bethel Lutheran Church in Chicago, identified yet another reason: "I can't suggest that the pastor serve as the executive director because the functions of that position can interfere with his 'being there' for people as a pastor. If as executive director, the pastor has to evict someone from a nonprofit-owned apartment for nonpayment of rent, for example, it will be hard for him to be a pastor to that family, to minister to them."

The Pastor as President

If the pastor is not serving as executive director for the reasons listed in the previous section, you may choose to ask him or her to serve as the president of the nonprofit. As described in the previous section, the president is much less involved in day-to-day operations of the nonprofit than the executive director, but still plays a key role in overseeing the big picture of the organization. In addition, the president may supervise the executive director and serve as a member of the nonprofit's board of directors.

While you could choose someone other than the pastor to serve as the president, there are some very good reasons for the pastor to fulfill this role:

- The nonprofit needs the pastor on its side in order to maintain the best possible relationship with the church. Having the pastor serve as president makes it easier to keep him or her in the loop about the needs and direction of the nonprofit. As a result, the pastor can be a more effective liaison for the nonprofit with church staff, lay leaders, and the larger congregation.

- As president of the nonprofit, the pastor can play a key role in endorsing the nonprofit to the congregation. Serving as president demonstrates a level of commitment to the nonprofit that the congregation may see as a stamp of approval. This may encourage the congregation to give more generously to the nonprofit, both in volunteer time and financial contributions.

- Serving as president will help the pastor more fully understand the realities of operating the nonprofit. He or she will be better able to respond to the nonprofit's needs and will be more likely to have realistic expectations about exactly what the nonprofit can do. For example, if the pastor sees exactly what it takes to secure major grants, he or she may be less likely to expect the nonprofit to double its budget in a short period.

The Pastor's Role in Supervising Nonprofit Staff

There are both advantages and risks to having the pastor supervise staff members of the nonprofit. Having the pastor supervise both church and nonprofit staff members can help both organizations work together more effectively. Having one person (the pastor) in the loop about who is doing what, may make it easier to coordinate programs and keep the missions of the two organizations aligned. If you are all reporting to the same person, meeting together at staff meetings, and so forth, it just makes it simpler to stay connected.

There is a significant downside, however, which is that many pastors simply do not have the time to supervise more people. Serving as pastor is a demanding job, and if your pastor is so busy that he or she cannot be available to staff members on a regular basis, you will probably want to consider a different kind of supervisory structure. The staff members of new organizations and programs frequently need more supervision at the outset as things are starting up. If the pastor is appointed supervisor and cannot provide the needed time, it will slow the development of the ministry and result in frustration for staff people and church members.

You will also need to assess whether your pastor has the expertise to supervise the staff for the new nonprofit. As described earlier in this chapter, many pastors do not have a nonprofit management background. Also, if the nonprofit is pursuing ministries that require staff with particular skills, such as a background in chemical dependency treatment or nursing, the pastor may not be qualified to serve as supervisor. In some states, certain types of social service programs, particularly those that serve vulnerable populations, are required to have supervisory staff with expertise in the field.

Asking the pastor to serve as supervisor could also be a problem if you have chosen to hire another person as executive director of the nonprofit. Keeping the pastor in the supervisory loop could undermine the authority of the executive director to manage the nonprofit—this can be frustrating and counterproductive for all of the staff members involved.

For example, if the executive director is responsible for overseeing program development, fundraising, and financial management for the organization, but is not responsible for staff supervision, everyone may become confused about who is really in charge. Program staff may feel divided between accountability to the executive director and the relationship with the pastor as supervisor. A strong case can be made for the executive director to assume responsibility for all of the day-to-day operations of the nonprofit, including staff supervision. In this case, the pastor would supervise only the executive director.

Hiring Processes

You will also need to decide whether the church will be involved in hiring staff for the nonprofit or not. Be sure to check out the rules of your denomination concerning this. The governing documents for your church may require the board or personnel committee of the church to be involved in hiring staff for any affiliated organizations.

Depending on how much control the church will have over the nonprofit (see chapter 5), you may want to include church leaders in hiring decisions in the following ways:

- approval of any new positions within the nonprofit
- approval of job descriptions and hiring processes
- approval of salary ranges and personnel policies
- giving the final "thumbs up" to recommended candidates
- involvement in disputes or disagreements between nonprofit staff and the executive director of the nonprofit or the nonprofit's board of directors
- vote on termination of staff

Hiring People from Your Church

Hiring someone from your church to work for the nonprofit could be the best or worst thing you ever do—from my experience, there does not seem to be much in-between. The perfect candidate for your job opening may be sitting in the pew on a Sunday morning, so be sure that you advertise position openings to your congregation members. You may be surprised about the kinds of experience and education that people in your church possess.

Church members can make excellent nonprofit staff members for a variety of reasons. They may have a higher level of commitment to the work of the nonprofit because they feel a sense of ownership for the ministry. Church members can also bring an understanding of church culture as well as relationships with other church members that may build a new program more quickly. When the congregation sees that "one of their own" is running a ministry, they become more inspired to participate by giving both their money and their time.

I have seen church-based nonprofits get into trouble with this when they hire church members who are unqualified or ill suited for a job. Sometimes churches are afraid to look outside the congregation for candidates because they do not want to attract someone with a different theology or religious background. Sometimes it just seems easier to hire people we know, rather than taking a chance on someone we do not. And it is less time consuming than a lengthy search process. I cannot be too blunt about this: do not hire people from your church solely for these reasons as I can almost guarantee you will regret it later.

Staff Sharing

It could be beneficial for the church and nonprofit to share staff members, but this needs to be negotiated carefully. For example, if neither organization can afford to hire a full-time youth worker, the two organizations could share one full-time staff person who does youth outreach. The cost of this position would then be split equally between the two organizations. One great benefit to hiring this way is that full-time positions generally attract higher quality candidates and inspire greater loyalty from employees.

Before you begin a staff sharing arrangement, always strive for clarity about:

- the number of hours the staff person will work for each organization
- who is supervising the staff person
- who pays them for which work
- times when one organization is to take precedence over the other (Sunday mornings, for example, or the launch of a major new nonprofit program)

There are two ways that new nonprofits might share staff with the sponsoring congregation:

One option is for current church staff members to put in some hours of work for the nonprofit, preferably on a paid basis (the church would be reimbursed for their time). The clerical staff of the church could provide five hours a week of support for the nonprofit, for example, or one of the pastors could devote part of her week to serving as the nonprofit's executive director.

The advantage for the nonprofit of sharing current church staff is that it can secure the human resources it needs without going out and hiring its own staff members. This is especially critical at the beginning of the nonprofit's life, when it may not have the resources to hire full-time (or even part-time) program or clerical staff. The disadvantage of this option is that church staff members may not have extra hours to devote to something new. If the members of the church office staff have all they can do to get the job done now, they probably are not in a position to say yes to working for the nonprofit.

A second option for sharing staff is that new staff members could be hired jointly by the church and the nonprofit. If neither organization can afford to hire a full-time music director, for example, the two organizations could pool their resources and hire one person, who would serve as music minister for the church half of the time and as the director of the nonprofit's community youth choir half of the time. Working together to offer full-time positions with benefits will enable both organizations to attract the kind of quality candidates they are seeking. "Our church was able to hire a full-time youth pastor because he worked half of the time for the nonprofit. We also hired a full-time custodian who worked half time for the nonprofit and half time for the church," said Rev. Sunny Kang, pastor of Woodland United Methodist Church in Duluth, and partnership advocate, Self-Development of People Committee, PCUSA.

A Key Part of the Recipe

There is no doubt that finding staff members who fit can be the difference between a nonprofit that achieves its mission and one that does not. But I believe there is more to it than that for congregations. If we believe that we are called to help people develop their giftedness and to find their place in the body of Christ, then we also have a great responsibility to the people we hire to work with us.

Of course, we will want to ensure that our staff members perform high quality work that meets our nonprofit's needs. But in addition, we are called to help employees have the best possible experience with our organization. Placing people in the right job opportunities is a key part of this, as is an emphasis on helping them grow and develop once we have hired them. Making personnel issues a key part of the discussion as you form your nonprofit will help you develop a personnel program that meets the needs of the nonprofit and its employees.

Key Questions

Personnel Issues

I.   Salary ranges and personnel policies

Will nonprofit staff be under the same salary ranges and personnel policies as the church staff?

If no, how will salary ranges for nonprofit staff be established?

How will nonprofit personnel policies differ from church personnel policies, and why?

II.   The Role of the Pastor

What is the role of the pastor with regard to the nonprofit?

Will the pastor manage the day-to-day operations of the nonprofit?

Will the pastor supervise nonprofit staff? If yes, which staff members?

III. Hiring Processes

Describe the hiring process for nonprofit staff members.

Will church staff or lay leaders be involved in any steps of the hiring process? If yes, how?

IV. Staff Sharing

Will the nonprofit and the church share any staff members?

If yes, develop job descriptions and schedules as follows:
- the amount of time devoted to working for each organization
- the duties of the employee while working for each organization
- the amount of the salary and benefits for which each organization will pay
- who will supervise the staff person

9

Legal Issues

Fourth Church of the Master has operated a food and clothing ministry for many years. Families come from communities near the church twice a week to receive food, household items, clothing, and furniture. During the past year, the staff of the outreach ministry has noticed a growing number of women in violent and abusive relationships coming to receive help.

The pastor of the church and chair of the outreach committee decide to research the resources available to battered women in their community. They find that the nearest women's shelter is 10 miles away and that there is frequently a waiting list for women to get in. Because of the limited resources available in the community and the enthusiasm for the project among a small group of volunteers within the church, the congregation decides to look seriously at opening a small women's shelter in a building adjacent to the church. A steering committee is formed of these volunteers, the outreach committee chair, a business executive who is a member of the church, and the senior pastor.

The idea to form a separate nonprofit (called Eve's Place) is seriously considered for several reasons. The cost of developing the building for the shelter is larger than the church's annual budget, and the church board wants the congregation to be protected from having to shoulder these expenses, particularly if there are unexpected costs in the development of the building. Also, the business executive on the steering committee works in the insurance industry, and she is concerned that working with a vulnerable population of women through the shelter will expose the church to new liability risks. A separate nonprofit could help insulate the church from lawsuits related to the operation of the new shelter.

Because funds are limited, several members of the steering committee volunteer to complete the legal paperwork for Eve's Place, rather than hiring an attorney. They successfully complete the application to become a nonprofit within their state. About three months after they file an application, the group receives an official-looking paper from their state's attorney general stating that it is now an official nonprofit.

The first foundation they approach for funding, however, informs them that they must also become a 501(c)(3) tax-exempt nonprofit through the federal government before most funders will consider making a gift to Eve's Place. After looking at the Internal Revenue Service forms that must be completed, one member of the steering committee suggests they seek help from his friend who is an attorney in bankruptcy law. Because the attorney has never worked with nonprofit organizations before, the Internal Revenue Service rejects his first two attempts at completing the forms. Finally, the steering committee finds an attorney specializing in nonprofit law through the United Way, and Eve's Place is recognized as tax exempt by the federal government about one year after the process of incorporating was begun.

You may have expected information on the legal process to be at the beginning of this book, where here it is near the end. When most people think of forming a nonprofit, they think only of the legal aspect. I have worked with many, many people in ministry who started the process of forming their organization by getting legal designation from the Internal Revenue Service—and then they thought they were done.

In reality, much work should go into forming an organization before any legal forms are filled out. A nonprofit organization has a mission, programs, staff and volunteers, a budget and fundraising goals, a board, and ways of interacting with the community. Going through the process of deciding some of these issues will help you make decisions about whether to legally incorporate and what type of legal designation would best fit your group and its mission.

Now that you have spent some time defining the mission of your new organization and choosing a board model, you are ready to make decisions about becoming the legal entity known as a 501(c)(3) nonprofit tax-exempt organization.

I will guide you through this process essentially in chronological order, beginning with a few more thoughts on what it means to be a nonprofit. I want to alert you now, however, to the two most common mistakes I have seen groups make. First, they do not realize that becoming a nonprofit is a two-part process: (1) your organization becomes legally recognized as a nonprofit organization in your own state (and any other states in which you operate) and (2) then you apply to be granted tax-exempt status by the IRS. These steps are discussed in detail later in this chapter (see page 123). Until you have completed both of the steps, your work is not done.

Another common error groups make in completing the legal process is that they do not spend enough time preparing to work with an attorney. Beginning on page 119, I provide a detailed outline of the steps you can take, before meeting with a legal expert, to make the best use of your time (and money) in this phase of your work.

What Does It Mean to Be a Nonprofit?

Nonprofit corporations are organized and operated under state law for religious, charitable, educational, literary, or scientific purposes. This definition includes all kinds of groups with a variety of purposes, all focused on benefiting the community in some way.

In order to qualify for tax-exempt status under Section 501(c)(3) of the Internal Revenue Code, a group must meet a few criteria:

1. The group must exist to benefit the community, not the people who run the organization. A nonprofit is different than a for-profit corporation, in which the profits (after bills are paid) are distributed among shareholders. In a nonprofit, the profits cannot be distributed to staff

or board members; instead, they are funneled back into the organization to be used to further benefit the community.

2. The group must avoid advocating for or against candidates for political office. It cannot substantially engage in influencing legislation or grassroots lobbying except as spelled out by federal regulations.

3. The group must use its assets to fulfill its mission. That is, the money, property, facilities and other assets of the nonprofit must be used to accomplish what it set out to do. If your group dissolves itself, the assets must be given to another 501(c)(3) nonprofit organization.

4. The group must receive most of its revenue from activities related to its charitable purposes. This means that most of the financial support comes through the "public support" of individuals, government, corporations and foundations, or through fees paid for products or services related to the organization's mission.

Legal Benefits of Incorporating as a Nonprofit

I have already covered some of the benefits of having a separate nonprofit at your church (see chapter 1), but there are additional legal benefits as well. Having a legally incorporated nonprofit as the umbrella for ministries helps provide a liability shield for the staff, board, and volunteers of the organization. Generally speaking, if the organization is sued, the organization bears the liability as long as the staff and board members acted without negligence.

Without the legal cover of the nonprofit, staff and board members might be required to pay damages out of their own pockets. For example, if a youth participating in your organization's canoe trip is seriously injured and his family decides to sue your group, not being incorporated as a nonprofit could mean that your staff and board members are responsible for paying legal fees and judgments.

Being tax exempt is a benefit in itself. Nonprofit tax-exempt organizations are exempt from corporate income tax and are eligible to apply for exemptions from other state and local taxes as well. Your group may be eligible for exemptions from the sales tax and property tax, for example, depending on the laws in your state. Being tax exempt can save you a great deal of money, freeing up additional resources to be put directly into the nonprofit's ministries; for example, you could save thousands of dollars every year by not having to pay sales tax on furniture, equipment, vehicles, and supplies.

It is important to note, however, that the tax exemption for nonprofits does not extend to payroll taxes. Your group will still have to pay FICA, unemployment, and state and federal withholding for each employee.

Becoming a tax-exempt nonprofit may also help you raise additional funds. Many funders are required by their own bylaws to make grants only to 501(c)(3) nonprofit organizations. Without that legal designation, your group may be foregoing support from funders who would otherwise be very interested in your programs.

In addition, incorporating brings a formality and structure to the organization that it would not otherwise have. This is essential when a group of people with differing opinions about what should be done and how to do it get together to run an organization. Your organizing documents, including the articles of incorporation and bylaws, provide you with a way to resolve disputes and delegate authority. This enables the nonprofit to stay focused on its overall mission instead of on disagreements among the people within the organization. Incorporating also helps the organization exist in perpetuity. Setting your organization up as a legal entity helps ensure that it will exist after the founding staff and board members have moved on.

The formality and structure of incorporation can also help provide your group with its own identity, making it more visible and attractive to funders, potential employees, volunteers, and collaborative partners.

Prepare for the Legal Process

By preparing for the legal process in advance, you will make the best use of the time and money you spend to go through the legal process. Before you even begin filling out forms or talking to an attorney, have the following things about your organization down in writing.

1. A clear mission statement for your organization that identifies it as having charitable intent. That is, the organization benefits the community, not just the people who run the organization. The clearer and more specific your statement, the better your chances of being approved for nonprofit status. Stating "we want to help the people of Central Heights"

is not as strong as "we want to help the children and youth of Central Heights succeed in school."

2. A financial plan that identifies where you think your funding for the organization will come from. Consider what part foundation grants, gifts from individual donors, fundraising events, and earned income will play in your overall financial picture.

3. A proposed three-year operating budget for the organization. This can be hard to develop from scratch, since you have no expenses yet to base it on. But do your best to calculate what you think the bottom line will be for each of the first three years of the organization's life.

4. Names of the people who will serve on the board of directors. All states have a minimum number of people that must serve on a board of directors. In the state of Minnesota, for example, a minimum of three people must serve on the board.

The Value of an Attorney

If you take nothing else from this chapter, I hope it is this: hiring an attorney to complete the legal process for you will be worth every penny. It will make the whole process smoother, faster, and less frustrating. You will also have a better chance of getting it right the first time.

Mary Nelson, president of Bethel New Life, a church-based nonprofit in Chicago, says that it is the first advice she gives to someone who is setting up a nonprofit at a church. She says, "With the litigious nature of our society, it's important to have some real expert advice about your bylaws, articles of incorporation, and compliance with IRS regulations. If you get it wrong, it's very hard to correct."

People always ask, "Can I complete the legal paperwork myself, without a lawyer?" The answer is, "Yes, probably." Your secretary of state's office can provide you with boilerplate forms, and you can also find them in a number of do-it-yourself legal books for nonprofits. The problem with doing it yourself is that if you are not an attorney, you probably will not know how to tailor the legal documents to meet the specific needs of your own organization.

For example, you will need to develop articles of incorporation and bylaws, and a number of issues might arise in that process. You will need to choose whether to be an organization that has voting members, which will be reflected in the bylaws. You may wish to require a two-thirds or three-quarters vote of your board to approve certain matters, instead of just requiring a simple majority. Your articles and bylaws may need to be tailored depending on the type of programs you offer or the funding you expect to receive. If you are organizing a school or are expecting to receive public grant monies, for example, the law may require you to add articles or bylaws related to nondiscrimination and preventing board members or staff from experiencing personal financial gain through grant funds.

Completing IRS Form 1023 (the one for federal tax-exempt status) can also be quite a challenge if you are working without an attorney. An attorney I know who works full time in nonprofit law said that he thinks this form is hard! The last time I checked, the form was 37 pages long, and required you to understand:

- the legal distinction between a private foundation and a public charity and which one you would like to be
- if you are becoming a public charity, the type you would like to become; for example, if you choose "church" you fall under a different set of requirements than if you choose "school, college or university" or "child care organization."
- what the legal phrase "disqualified person" means and who in your organization meets that definition
- whether you are engaged in "unrelated business activities" and what those will be

If any of the above phrases are confusing to you, you probably need legal help in preparing Form 1023.

An attorney can also advise you on employment law issues. Depending on the size of your organization, you may be obligated to conform to certain employment regulations after you incorporate, such as the Family Medical Leave Act. I describe what to look for in an attorney and how to find one in the next section of this chapter.

How to Locate an Attorney

Once you have prepared your group for the legal process, look for an attorney with nonprofit law experience, preferably someone who has filed incorporation and tax-exemption paperwork for other nonprofits. It might be possible for a lawyer without a nonprofit law background to complete this process for you, but it could take a lot longer. Also, working with a nonprofit attorney will help ensure that the paperwork is filled out correctly the first time. This helps you avoid lengthy delays.

Some attorneys will do *pro bono* work for nonprofits; that is, they work for free or at a discounted rate. Many law firms around the country have set a standard for themselves to donate a certain percentage of their billable hours to the community. Ask attorneys you connect with if they would be willing to do the work *pro bono*. Here are some places where you might find an attorney:

1. Your own congregation. Be sure to let your own members know you are looking for an attorney—there might be an attorney or someone who is related to one sitting right in the pews. There may also be legal assistants or others who could get you connected with an attorney at the law firm where they work.
2. Neighborhood legal clinics. Some communities (typically lower-income ones) have legal clinics that provide free or deeply discounted legal advice. If there is one of these in your community, stop by to see if the attorneys there might be able to help you.
3. Partner churches. You may want to approach a current partner church to see if there are any attorneys there who could help. Also, check out churches in your own denomination.
4. Local legal organizations. Your local or state bar association may connect attorneys to volunteer opportunities. There may also be a separate organization, such as the Volunteer Lawyers Network, that does this.
5. Your local United Way. The United Way may be able to connect you with people or groups in your community that help nonprofits complete the legal process. Ask the United Way if there is a nonprofit group in your area that places management volunteers or board members. In Minnesota, Management Assistance Project (MAP) sends out volunteers with particular management expertise to nonprofit groups.

MAP also has an attorney on staff who completes the legal paperwork for nonprofits for a small fee.
6. Local colleges or universities. The nonprofit management program at a local college or university (often located within the business school) may have connections with nonprofit attorneys as well.
7. Other nonprofits. Check with other nonprofits in your area to find out which law firms or attorneys they have used.

Steps in the Legal Process

As you work with your attorney, it will be helpful for you to understand the steps in the legal process. Becoming a tax-exempt organization is a two-part process. First, your organization becomes legally recognized as a nonprofit organization in your own state (and any other states in which you operate); then you apply to be granted tax-exempt status by the IRS. One note: Legislation is introduced periodically in Congress that would streamline the application process for becoming a nonprofit. Your attorney can provide you with the most current information on the steps involved in the process.

Here is a very brief summary of the current steps involved in becoming a nonprofit tax-exempt organization:

Becoming an Incorporated Nonprofit Organization in Your State

1. Name your organization.
   First choose a name for your organization, then check if the name is being used by anyone else in your state. In many states, you can find out if the name you chose is available by looking on the secretary of state's Web site. Once your articles of incorporation are accepted by the secretary of state (see step 2 below), the name is yours. If you think it will be awhile before you file your articles, however, you may want to consider reserving the name so that no one else can use it. If the name is not being used by another organization and is not confusingly similar to a name already in use, you can reserve it through the secretary of state's office. One note: If your group intends to operate in more than one state, you will need to reserve the name in each of those states.

2.   Prepare the articles of incorporation.
     This is the document that brings your organization into existence as a
     nonprofit entity within your state. Once your articles of incorporation
     are accepted by the secretary of state's office in your state, you can
     say "we are now in business as a nonprofit in (your state) as of this
     date." Your state will have specific requirements for the articles of
     incorporation, and your attorney should be able to tell you what they
     are. Generally, your articles of incorporation will include the name and
     purpose of the nonprofit; the number, names, and addresses of the first
     board of directors; and the name and address of at least one person
     who serves as an incorporator for the nonprofit. Usually the incorporator
     is a member of the first board of directors, but normally any person
     may be designated as the incorporator. There are other provisions in
     the articles as well, and your attorney will check state law for you to
     determine what else you need to include.

3.   File the articles of incorporation with your secretary of state.

4.   Prepare your bylaws.
     The bylaws are like the "rule book" for the day-to-day operations of
     your organization. They detail specific procedures for how the
     organization conducts its business. Issues covered in the bylaws
     typically include:

     • Whether the organization is a membership or nonmembership
       organization. You need to decide whether your group will have
       legal voting members who have rights that include electing the
       board of directors and approving changes to the articles or bylaws
       of the corporation. Most nonprofits choose a nonmembership
       structure.
     • How board members and officers are elected and how long they
       serve.
     • When meetings are held and how often.
     • A committee structure for the organization.
     • How the church is involved in governing the nonprofit; for example,
       if the church board has the right to review and sign off on certain
       types of decisions made by the nonprofit, these should be detailed
       in the bylaws of the nonprofit.

Becoming a 501(c)(3) Tax-Exempt Organization as Recognized by the Federal Government

If you complete only the first four steps outlined above, your organization will not be tax exempt. This means that your group will have to pay taxes, and contributions to it will not be tax deductible. The second step, requesting 501(c)(3) tax-exempt status from the IRS, involves completing Form 1023, the lengthy application I mentioned earlier in this chapter. The form requires you to fully describe the activities, finances, and governance of your proposed nonprofit organization. If you are approved as a nonprofit, tax-exempt organization by the IRS, your organization may become eligible to apply for exemption from state income tax, sales tax, and property tax, depending on the laws of your state.

5. Prepare Form 8718: User Fee for Exempt Organization Determination Letter Request.
   This form is used to calculate the fee you will pay for filing Form 1023. The fee will be either $150 or $500, depending on the average gross receipts of your group during the past four years; that is, the donations and revenue received by your organization.

6. Prepare tax-exemption application: Form 1023.
   This is the application that asks the federal government to recognize your group as tax exempt under Section 501(c)(3). (One important note: churches themselves are not required to complete IRS Form 1023 in order for the church congregation to become a tax-exempt organization. If you develop a nonprofit that is separate from your church, however, you will need to complete this form.)

7. Prepare Form SS-4: Application for Employer Identification Number.

Other Registrations or Applications to Be Completed

8. Receive a state corporate income tax exemption.
   Most states have some form of corporate income tax. Now that you are considered tax exempt by the federal government, you will probably be exempt from state corporate income tax as well, depending on the laws in your state. You may need to submit a copy of your tax filing (Form 990) to the state to receive the exemption.

Form 990 is the annual Return of Organization Exempt from Income Tax. Many tax-exempt nonprofits are required to submit this form to the IRS each year, but there are some notable exceptions. Consult with your attorney to find out if your group is required to complete the form. The form includes many specific questions about your organization, but briefly, you will be required to disclose revenue, assets, and expenses; any changes in governance; and information about income-producing activities. There is also a Statement of Program Services Accomplishments in which you describe the number of participants and services or products delivered.

9. Apply for other tax exemptions; for example, state sales tax and property tax.

10. Meet other registration requirements.
    Some states and localities require nonprofits to register with the attorney general's office or another state office. Typically, you will have to submit budgets, audits, and information on your fundraising activities within the state.

11. Obtain solicitation licenses.
    Some states and localities require that nonprofits obtain a solicitation license if they are raising funds above a certain amount or from the public generally.

Timelines and Costs

You need to know that becoming a nonprofit tax-exempt organization can be a lengthy process. Several attorneys I spoke to about the length of the legal process said that it is not unusual for an organization to receive tax-exempt status about one year after Form 1023 is submitted to the IRS. So include this waiting period in your plans and timelines as you work to set up your organization.

Once you have submitted your application and are waiting for a response from the IRS, your group is allowed to act like a tax-exempt organization in two respects: you are not required to pay corporate income taxes, and contributions to your group are tax deductible. If your application is rejected by the IRS, however, your nonprofit will be required to pay taxes on all of the income received to that point.

Fiscal Agents

You may want to consider using a fiscal agent to receive grants and donations on your behalf while you are waiting for your nonprofit status, particularly if the funders you are approaching prefer to deal with an organization that has already received its 501(c)(3) status. One important note: in order for a fiscal agent to provide this service legally, the fiscal agent must own the funds and not merely be a conduit for them. There is, however, an exception for government grant funds. Work with your attorney to develop a written agreement with your fiscal agent that meets the requirements of the law.

In selecting a fiscal agent, you will want to look for a group that is large enough to have bookkeeping capacity. You might approach a large, well-established social service agency in your area about serving as your fiscal agent. Neighborhood groups or networking organizations may also play this role for you. You will typically pay a fee to the fiscal agent for the service they provide. In my experience working in Minnesota, it is not unusual for a fiscal agent to ask for 5 to 10 percent of a total budget or grant as a fee. Be sure to put your agreement with the fiscal agent down in writing: their fee, what they are to deliver, and the specific timelines under which they are operating.

Fees

In addition to any fees you pay your attorney, you will pay fees to the IRS and your secretary of state's office for the privilege of becoming a nonprofit. Fees paid to the secretary of state or another state office that handles nonprofit incorporations should be fairly minimal. In Minnesota, they are less than $100.

Currently, the IRS charges either $150 or $500 for the process of becoming a 501(c)(3) tax-exempt nonprofit. The fee your organization is charged depends on the average annual gross receipts during the first four years of its existence. The fee is sent along with your application for tax-exempt status.

Other Legal Issues

You may also want to be aware of the following legal issues. If you think any of these might affect your organization, ask your attorney for advice on next steps.

1. Send receipts to donors. The IRS requires donors who make financial contributions of $250 or more in one calendar year to have a written acknowledgment of the gift. The acknowledgment you send to donors can be in the form of a thank-you letter that includes the amount and when it was given. The IRS likes to see language like this on a receipt: "This donation was not made in exchange for any gifts or services." This makes it clear that the money sent was a donation, rather than a payment for a product or a fee for a service.

2. Determine whether you owe unrelated business tax. You may have to pay unrelated business income tax (UBIT) on income you generate for your nonprofit if what you do to get the money is not directly related to your mission as a tax-exempt organization. Often this involves selling products or services to the public. This tax also takes effect if too large a percentage of your revenue comes from these activities.

    If your nonprofit's mission is to "build the skills of community youth," for example, then the sales of furniture made by the youth would probably not be subject to this tax, since the process of making the furniture benefited the youth. On the other hand, if your youth-serving organization has an annual sale selling "seconds" from local furniture factories and the youth are not involved at all, you may very well have to pay UBIT on the proceeds since the sale itself was not related to your mission.

    Check out any income-generating activities with your attorney or accountant first, to see if you might have to pay UBIT on the proceeds. You may need to hire a professional with specialized skills to help you sort this out.

3. Become familiar with limits on political lobbying. If your nonprofit has the desire to be involved in political campaigns, then tread lightly. There are strict IRS regulations about the amount of political lobbying that a nonprofit can do and still retain its tax-exempt status.

    Tax-exempt nonprofits are not allowed to engage in political campaigns for or against particular candidates for political office. In addition, there are limits on how much a tax-exempt nonprofit can be involved in grassroots political lobbying on behalf of particular political issues or legislation. Your attorney can spell out for you the limits on the amount of staff time and money that can be used for this (it depends on the size of your organization).

If one of your organization's goals is to get people involved in the political process, there are many ways you can do this without violating IRS rules. Efforts to register voters or educate the public about issues (as long as you do not advocate for one viewpoint) are considered okay, as are candidate forums that invite all of the candidates for a particular office.

4. Trademark the name of your organization. If you think your group will expand so that its services will be provided outside of your local community, you may want to consider securing a registered trademark for your name. If you are the first organization to obtain a federally registered trademark, no one else can use your name in a confusingly similar way. A trademark can protect both the name itself and the way it is presented graphically; for example, in a logo or particular design. There is a cost to the process of trademarking your name—the attorney I worked with on this chapter estimated that it costs about $1,500 and takes at least a year.

5. Register a domain name for a Web site. If setting up your own Web site will be critical to the work of your group, you may want to check the Internet domain names that are available before you choose a name for your group. You can check the availability of names online at various Web sites including www.whois.net. You can also register a name at that site.

You may also want to check out domain names that are similar to yours—ones that the public may assume are connected to your organization. For example, if you register godswork.org, you may also want to register godswork.com. There have been several well-documented cases of similar domain names being used by businesses that ministry groups would definitely not want to be associated with.

6. Purchase liability insurance for the nonprofit. Once your group has begun operating, it will need its own liability insurance. Do not assume that the church's policy will cover the activities of the new nonprofit—it might not. Talk to your insurance agent early in the process of forming your nonprofit to discuss the type and amount of insurance you will need. Also, get an estimate of the cost so you can put it in your proposed budget for the nonprofit.

Legal Issues Checklist

Check when completed	Who will do it	Date to be completed

Select an Attorney

Identify organizations or firms to check with:

1.
2.
3.
4.
5.

Prepare for the Legal Process

____ Develop a clear mission
____ Develop a three-year budget
____ Identify board members
____ Identify where funding will come from

Steps in the Legal Process

____ Select a name for your group
____ Develop the articles of incorporation
____ File the articles of incorporation
____ Prepare the bylaws
____ Prepare Form 8718:
____ User Fee for Exempt Organization
____ Determination Letter Request

(continued)

Check when completed	**Who will do it**	**Date to be completed**

Prepare Form 1023:
Tax Exemption Application
___ Prepare Form SS-4:
Application for Employer Identification Number
___ Apply for other tax exemptions
  • state income tax
  • state sales tax
  • state property tax
  • other taxes
___ Meet other registration requirements for your state
  1.
  2.
  3.

Other Legal Issues
___ Purchase liability insurance for the nonprofit
___ Set up a system to send receipts to donors
___ Check with your attorney about unrelated business income tax
___ Check with your attorney about limits on political lobbying
___ Trademark the name of your organization (optional)
___ Register the domain name of your Web site (optional)

10

Successful Fundraising

"There were so many things we assumed about fundraising as we were forming our nonprofit," said one particularly discouraged executive director. "We assumed we were going to go directly to congregation members for donations in support of the nonprofit, but this request was denied by the pastor. He was concerned about money being diverted from church giving. We assumed that our board members would ask all of their friends for funds, but most were too uncomfortable to do that. And we assumed that it would be easy to secure gifts from foundations and corporations in our community. These funders, however, were concerned that we were brand new and had no track record. All of these assumptions set us back about a year in the launching of our programs. I wish we would have talked about our fundraising plan from the very beginning."

When I first put together the outline for this book, there was no chapter on fundraising. I figured there were many books that had already been written on the topic, and I did not need to write any more. My friends who run church-based nonprofits, however, insisted I include fundraising in the book. Many of them identified this as a key issue that was left out of initial discussions about forming the nonprofit, causing their organizations to suffer as they attempted to move forward.

Many people find fundraising to be one of the more uncomfortable aspects of running an organization. People in my fundraising classes frequently describe asking for money as embarrassing, guilt producing, and just plain hard. This discomfort causes many new organizations to leave fundraising out of the conversation as they are forming themselves. While our human nature and our cultural baggage may make us feel uncomfortable about fundraising, I do not think that this discomfort is from God. Jesus was unafraid to discuss money—many of his parables focus on stewardship of resources. I was also surprised to find that the process of securing resources is described in detail in a number of biblical passages, both in the Old and New Testament. We get the strong message from the Bible that we are not to be afraid to talk about money and that resource development is a legitimate part of the ministry.

So while fundraising may be a difficult topic for you to discuss as you work to form your new nonprofit, I would encourage you to proceed with as detailed a conversation as possible on the topic. Identifying who will raise the money, how much you need, and which sources will likely provide the support will help you secure the resources you need more quickly.

I begin this chapter with a list of ideas about how your church and the people in it can provide resources for the nonprofit. Once you secure support there, you will be much more successful when you approach outside funders, such as corporations and private foundations in your community. Outside funders will want to see that the people closest to the organization support it before they will consider making grants.

Seek Ye First within Your Own Congregation

"Look within your own congregation first," is always the advice I give to congregations that are launching a new nonprofit, and without exception, the response is something like: "What! Ask within our own congregation? That's why we're setting up the nonprofit, so we can get foundation grants and forget about bothering our own people for money."

The truth is, the financial support from your congregation will be key to leveraging all other kinds of support that you will draw into the nonprofit. Even if your church congregation is composed of people with very few financial resources, if church members give sacrificially to support the work of the nonprofit, it will convince foundations, corporations, and government funders to give more generously.

Think about it—if you were a foundation considering a request from your church-based nonprofit, wouldn't you want to know what the church was putting into it? "How much does the church give?" was always one of the first questions I was asked when any outside funder came for a site visit. When I could answer that church members provided generous financial gifts and over 10,000 hours of volunteer service each year, many funders took our organization more seriously, and I believe the strong support of church members led to many more gifts from supporters outside the church.

While I served at Park Avenue, we always made an annual appeal to the congregation to support the summer ministry for youth. The appeal was done by the Park Avenue Foundation through letters, bulletin inserts, and announcements from the pulpit. I always told the congregation that we needed every gift, and the gifts always came in a huge range—from several dollars to several thousand. One year a little boy came running up to me after the Sunday service and gave me two quarters. He said: "This is my allowance for the week, and I want you to have it so you can help some kids go to camp." You better believe I told that story to the largest foundation in the state when they came for a site visit that fall.

Another story I love to tell is of the elderly woman who put two dollars in the offering plate every single week, designated for our health clinic that provided free care to people without health insurance. She was one of the least economically privileged people in our congregation, so her gift was a sacrificial one for her. She gave generously because she knew what it was like to go without.

How and When to Ask Your Church Members

There are many ways to ask your church members for their support. The first step should be for the nonprofit to coordinate its appeal with key staff at the church, particularly the senior pastor. Many churches have an approval process for how and when church members are asking for money—do not surprise everybody by just "winging" a request on a Sunday morning. Your church may have very spontaneous Sunday services, but from my experience, most people do not like surprises when it comes to money.

Strategize about a time(s) during the year when the nonprofit could ask without competing with other ministries (this may not be possible if you are making a year-end appeal). If the church's trustee board makes an appeal every Easter for capital projects, you might want to ask for support for the nonprofit at another time. Prime times during the year for a church-based nonprofit to ask include:

1. Any time of the year when you are about to launch a program. If you do special summer programming, for example, begin asking the congregation for support in April. People will respond to the need and to the excitement of making something happen quickly through their financial gifts.
2. The end of the calendar year. This is a time when other ministries will be asking too, so you will need to coordinate your appeal. So many people make their giving decisions at the end of the calendar year that it would be a missed opportunity not to ask sometime during the last six weeks of the year.

Methods of Asking

A good rule of thumb about asking for money: people need to receive something in writing *and* they need to hear about the opportunity, either during a Sunday morning service or through a face-to-face conversation. We wish that people in our church would pick up the phone or write out a check just because they received a mailing. The truth is, most of us just let these written requests drift to the bottom of the pile. We need someone to remind us about the opportunity. A few ways to ask include:

1. Send a letter to the congregation asking for their support of the nonprofit. Be sure to include an easy way for people to respond—usually a pledge card and return envelope. People love to see how their gift makes a difference, so you may want to break down gift sizes into what each gift could accomplish; for example, $25 sends one child to a week of day camp, $200 sponsors one child in the tutoring class, or $500 buys health care for 10 people.
2. Include a bulletin insert asking for support. Include a pledge card and return envelope inside the bulletin, or design a special insert with pledge categories and information on it. Photos or graphics will draw people's attention.
3. Make an appeal from the pulpit during the Sunday morning service. It is the time during the week when the largest group of church members is sitting right in front of you. Make the most of it. This is most effective when there is a pledge card or insert in the bulletin that Sunday. When you make your announcement, hold up the pledge card or insert and ask people to drop it in the offering plate.

4. Make face-to-face contacts with key donors within your congregation. These types of requests are best made by a peer—someone else in the congregation who is well known by the person you are asking.

5. Ask church members to give to your nonprofit through the federated drive they give to at work. The United Way is the best known of these, but there are many others as well. A number of these programs now allow people to designate their gifts to nonprofits, even if the nonprofit is not a member of the federation. If this is allowed in your area, get the forms that are required and distribute them within your congregation.

From my experience, this is a very effective way to raise money, since so many people are "strongly encouraged" to support federated drives at work and feel somewhat frustrated by the kinds of agencies that their gift supports. This option gives them a choice and provides you with additional funds for the nonprofit.

Securing Corporate Grants through Your Congregation Members

People in your congregation may be your greatest asset in securing grants from corporations. Corporations set up contributions programs to be good citizens in the communities where they are located, to promote a good feeling about the company among the people of the area. They love to fund projects that significantly involve their employees. In fact, some require that employees be involved with an organization before a grant is made to it.

If you can find out where the people in your congregation are employed, you can call on them to put in a good word for the nonprofit as you are submitting a grant proposal to the corporation where they work. Your chances of securing a grant will increase if that person is involved with the nonprofit as a program volunteer or board member. Corporations would love to promote the fact that their employees are tutoring children, building affordable housing, or feeding the hungry.

It used to be that companies would make grants mainly to nonprofits that their CEO and vice presidents were involved with, but this is no longer the case. Many companies are encouraging all of their employees to get involved in the community, and the grant dollars are following them. So even if your church is filled with factory workers, scientists, office managers, or computer specialists, if they work for a major corporation they can probably increase your chances of getting a grant.

Try to find some creative ways to find out where your church members are employed. You may need to be sensitive about gathering employment information if your church has a large number of unemployed people, but try to stress that everyone has something to contribute to the work of the nonprofit, and making connections with corporations is one of the many ways people can help.

When I worked at Park Avenue, we put an insert in the bulletin that said, "We Want to Ask You a Personal Question," which caught people's attention. Folks filled in their name, employer, and phone number and dropped the insert into the offering plate. This information helped us secure several grants from major corporations and connected us with a vice president of a major corporation in town. We were not even aware she was in our own congregation.

You could also ask for employment information on church directory forms or applications for church membership. Then whenever you identify a potential new corporate funder, you could search the church database for employees of that company.

Other Ways Your Congregation Can Help

As you are asking your congregation to give generously to the nonprofit, do not forget that there are many other ways to give support than simply writing a check. For example:

1. In-kind gifts of products and services can be a great boost to the work of the nonprofit. Business owners in your congregation or employees of major corporations may be able to secure this type of donation. The list of possible donations is almost endless: computer equipment and software, food, printing services, vehicles, athletic and camping equipment, books and curriculum, school supplies, medicine, and lumber and other construction materials. If you need something, get the word out to people and you may be surprised who steps forward to help. One caution: do not accept items that are not in good working order or that cannot be used by your organization. For example, obsolete computer systems may be offered to you on a regular basis.

Accepting them may make the donor feel good, but you will have to waste your valuable time getting rid of the things.

2. Donations of property or facilities. There may be people in your congregation who own land or facilities that they want to donate to somebody—why not ask them to give to your nonprofit? These donations provide a tax break for the donor and could provide you with cash for programs if you decide to sell the donated property. The donation could also provide the space you need for your offices or new programs, depending on where it is located.

    Before accepting donations of property, have the land and facility inspected by a knowledgeable person from the construction industry. They may be able to spot the need for costly renovations. They will also know how to look for damage to the land that would require you to spend a great deal of money on cleanup (such as a leaking underground oil tank). Also, have an attorney work with you to determine if there are any financial or tax obligations attached to the property. You do not want to find out later that there are back property taxes or a $6,000 water bill due.

3. Deferred gifts. Ask church members to consider putting the nonprofit in their will. This is an easy way to secure financial support for the future of the organization. There are other ways for your members to make planned gifts as well. These can provide income to the nonprofit either now or later, after the death of the donor. One easy way to promote this idea is to ask a financial professional within your church to offer an estate-planning seminar free of charge to your members (or for a small fee). This will be a valuable service for the congregation and will help encourage people to consider making deferred gifts.

4. Donations of professional expertise. People in your congregation who can give of their professional expertise can help you reduce your budget for legal advice, accounting services, graphic design, and photography (just to name a few). You may find an accountant who is willing to complete the annual audit for the nonprofit at a much-reduced fee, for example, or a graphic designer who will do the layout for your annual report for free.

Support Directly from the Church

In addition to asking individuals within your congregation for support, consider what the church itself might provide for the launch of the nonprofit. You may be able to secure funds from the church budget directly or through in-kind donations. As mentioned previously in this chapter, any support from the church will help you leverage dollars from outside the church.

As the nonprofit gets grants and gifts from outside your church, you may want to consider paying the church for some of the items listed below. Paying the church could prove to be a cheaper route than buying or leasing the items for the exclusive use of the nonprofit. Paying the church for the use of the copy machine, for example, would probably cost less than leasing a machine for use only by the nonprofit.

You might also want to consider paying the church staff to put a certain number of hours per week towards the work of the nonprofit, at least when you first launch the organization. If the nonprofit needs just a few hours of help each week, it is more difficult to go out and hire someone to do a small amount of work for a small amount of money. If five hours of clerical help and two hours of janitorial support would make all the difference, see if you can pay church staff for that small amount of time. Working out arrangements with staff must be negotiated with the church, of course, and the staff involved must be clear whom they are reporting to. (See the Staff Sharing section in chapter 8, pp. 111-112.)

Some options to consider for support from the church include:

1. A line-item donation from the church budget. Depending on the size of your church and its financial state, it may be possible to secure start-up funds or ongoing support for the work of the nonprofit. Educate yourself about the budgeting process of the church—find out who to approach, when to ask, and what they will need in writing in order to consider your request.
2. Financial support from committees of the church or service groups. Committees within your church may have funds to give away that are outside of the regular church budget. Check with the social concerns, mission, or outreach committees, or other committees related to the work you want to do. Small groups or service groups may also be able to support you financially. The seniors group, women's circle, or small

group Bible studies may take a regular offering that they use to support projects of the church.

3. Donation of office and program space. Using space free of charge can save you a bundle as you launch your new organization. Starting out, for example, the executive director of the nonprofit could be housed in the church offices, and the tutoring program could operate in a classroom in the church basement.

4. Donation of church staff time. As you launch the nonprofit, there may not be money to hire an executive director. Perhaps one of the pastors of the church would be willing to take the helm while still on the church's payroll. Church program staff could donate time to help develop curriculum, teach classes, recruit and train volunteers, and other tasks related to getting the programs up and running.

5. Donation of supplies and equipment. Can you use one of the church's computers for nonprofit business? How about the copying and postage machines? Ask the church whether they would share office supplies too.

6. Use of vehicles. If you need to transport participants or volunteers for the nonprofit's programs, ask if you can use the church's vehicles. Make sure you have the right liability and vehicle insurance for the nonprofit before you use any vehicles for your programming.

7. Vehicle and liability insurance. You will need it for your nonprofit activities and it can be expensive. See if the church is willing to add the nonprofit to its policy and cover the cost for a while.

Approaching Foundations and Corporations

Once you have secured support from the church connected to the nonprofit, you will be in a much stronger position to go out and ask local foundations and corporations for funding. This is another huge topic. Look at the bibliography in this book for resources that will provide much more detailed information than space here allows.

To prepare for submitting grants, you will want to take the following steps.

1. Hire a fundraising consultant or development director (see pp. 105-106) to plan and implement a fundraising strategy for the nonprofit that includes funding from foundations and corporations.

2. If you do not hire a consultant or development director, send a person from the nonprofit, preferably someone who has strong writing skills and the time to work on grants, to a class on grant writing. The classes will probably be offered through the nonprofit management-training center at a local college or university (often a part of the business school) or through continuing education. Your local United Way may offer them as well, or the professional association in your state that serves either nonprofit organizations or foundations.
3. Research local funders that support organizations similar to yours. Your local library may have indexes of foundations and corporations in your area. Also, call groups that are similar to yours and get copies of their annual reports—there will frequently be a list of donors included.
4. Secure information on funders you would like to approach. Many foundations and corporations issue written guidelines and annual reports describing what they will and will not give to (many offer these on their Web sites as well). Guidelines will tell you the program and geographic focus of the funder as well as what to include in a grant proposal. Get a copy and study it.

Elements of a Winning Grant Proposal

Many people see grant writing as some sort of magic skill that only a few humans possess. The truth is, if you can write, you can write a grant. Grant writing is simply persuasive writing to convince a funder that your organization is worthy of support.

What should you put in your grant proposal? That depends entirely on who is being asked for money. Many foundations and corporations have prepared written guidelines for their giving programs. If you read and understand the guidelines and write your proposal accordingly, you will have a much greater chance of getting funded.

In some states, foundation and corporate funders have put together a common grant application form that all of the funders in the area accept. Check with your local United Way or an association of nonprofits to see if funders from your area have developed a common grant application. There may also be a professional association for local funders, like the Minnesota Council on Foundations, that can provide you with information on what the funders in your area prefer.

Typically, the following information will need to be in your grant proposal.

Format for a Grant Proposal

Information on your organization. Be sure to include:
- name, address, and phone number
- contact person
- brief history of your organization

Mission and goals. State succinctly what it is that you are trying to do. Funders like mission statements that demonstrate a sharp focus on what it is you are trying to do. Also list major goals of the organization, both in programming and management. For example, you might state "goals for the coming year" and list "develop a welfare to work training program for 25 women" and "increase special events revenue by 25 percent."

A description of current programs with number of participants listed. Briefly describe current programs, being sure to point out their results. Include success stories of participants, being sure to change names in order to protect confidentiality.

Recent accomplishments. Do not forget to sing your own praises! Let the funder know what you have accomplished in the past year—program successes as well as how the organization has strengthened itself. Did you begin any new programs? Did you raise additional funds, begin new partnerships, develop a strategic plan?

The amount of money you are asking for and how it will be used. In my experience, the most common complaint of funders is: "They didn't tell me what they wanted!" Be sure to ask for a specific amount, and describe how the funds will be used.

A demonstrated need and a description of the community you are serving. Educate the funder about your community. What is the geographic area like? Who are the people you are attempting to serve?

Program description. Here is your opportunity to explain your program idea fully. State the goals and objectives clearly. Also, demonstrate that you have thought through the steps it will take to implement the program. Funders will look for a clear plan that spells out who is responsible for various aspects of the program and the timeline for implementation. A housing program might have the goal of "develop four homes for purchase by low-income families." Some of the steps involved might include: secure property and financing, select contractors and recruit volunteers, implement renovation process, select families, and host celebration event.

Collaboration. List the organizations and people you are partnering with to implement the ministry and describe how you are working with them. Funders love to see that you are aware of what else is happening in your community, and that you are working with others to share resources. So if you are working with the public schools, the block clubs, the ministerial alliance, or local businesses, be sure to describe those partnerships in your grant. Some funders will not make grants to organizations that do not collaborate.

Qualifications of key staff members. This usually involves listing the biographies of the executive director, president, and appropriate program director. Funders want to see that your staff members have the skills and experience to carry out your organization's mission. Make sure to include program expertise as well as management skills.

An evaluation plan. Describe how you will measure the impact of your program on the people who participate in it. "Outcomes measurement" has become the battle cry of funders everywhere. They want to see more than just a need in the community; they want you to document that you are making a difference in the lives of the people you are working to serve. Typically, you will include a list of program outcomes as well as the methods you will use to measure whether the outcomes were achieved; for example, tests, surveys, and interviews.

Attachments to the grant proposal. Depending on what the funder is asking for, you may want to include:
- proof that your organization has been legally incorporated as a nonprofit (your 501(c)(3) letter from the IRS)
- a program budget
- an annual audit of the nonprofit's finances
- a list of board members and their affiliations
- the most recent newsletter or annual report of the nonprofit
- other attachments, as requested by the funder

Other Sources of Funding

So many organizations focus on the big grants from foundations and corporations that they may forget about other possible sources of funding— some of these may be easy for you to tap into. Consider seeking support from:

1. Individual donors within and outside of your church. Individuals donate most of the money given to charitable organizations in the United States.
2. Government grants. State, local, and federal funds may be available for a variety of programs including day care, housing and economic development, youth programming, and job training.
3. Other churches, both within your own denomination and outside of it.
4. Your denomination. Some denominations have special funds set aside for social justice advocacy, economic development, programs responding to hunger, programming for women and people of color, and other special projects.
5. Small businesses in the neighborhood where your ministry operates might provide small financial donations or in-kind gifts.
6. Other larger nonprofits. Some larger nonprofits may be looking to subcontract with smaller organizations to deliver services.
7. Professional or trade associations. Associations such as your local bar association, medical association, and so forth, might offer support as well. The bar association could help you get your legal clinic started, for example, or an association for medical workers might be interested in your proposed healthcare program.
8. Neighborhood associations or block clubs. These associations or clubs may have secured funding to be dispersed to groups in the neighborhood. If they have a large grant for youth programming, for example, the neighborhood association may be looking to groups like yours to actually develop the program and recruit youth.
9. Service clubs or fraternal organizations. Service clubs or fraternal organizations, such as the Lions Club, Jaycees, or VFW, are often good sources of funding.

Put the "Fun" in Fundraising

While fundraising can be a challenging and all-consuming task, I hope you also find it fun. Some of the most rewarding and enjoyable experiences I have had in the ministry have involved developing relationships with funders. It really can be fun to get to know a person, understand their interests and passions, and then match those with the vision of your organization. In general, I think many people in the ministry come with less experience in fundraising than folks who work in other types of nonprofits; however, do not be discouraged by your lack of experience. The good news is that your ministry background has equipped you to effectively build relationships with people, and that is the key to successful fundraising. Funders are people, and if you truly work to listen to them and understand them, you will not only make new friends but will also develop new donors.

Key Questions about Fundraising

Who will be responsible for raising funds for the nonprofit?

What type of training and support will they need to raise the necessary funds?

Where will you get start-up funding for the initial costs of forming the nonprofit?

How will the church itself support the work of the nonprofit financially?

Will the nonprofit be allowed to ask the members of the congregation for financial support? If yes, how often?

How will the members be approached; for example, by letter, announcement, or face-to-face meetings?

Which types of funders will you approach?
Check all that apply:

_____ members of your congregation
_____ other churches
_____ your denomination
_____ corporations
_____ foundations
_____ government agencies
_____ small businesses
_____ individual donors
_____ professional groups or trade associations
_____ service clubs or fraternal groups
_____ other larger nonprofits
_____ the neighborhood association or block club

Next Steps

1. Take each category of funder you selected and estimate the amount of money you think you can raise from each in the nonprofit's first year.
2. Under each category, list specific people or organizations you would like to approach for funding (i.e., Mary and Richard Johnson, the Ford Foundation, First Bank, Target Corporation).
3. Develop a strategy for each possible funder:
   - amount to ask for
   - potential interest in your organization (in the case of corporate or foundation funders, read their guidelines and annual reports)
   - the best person to ask them (friends and business colleagues are often good choices)
   - the best time of the year to ask

11

Maintaining a Positive Relationship with Your Church

Once the nonprofit is up and running, it may seem like your work with the church is over; but really, it is just beginning! While it is possible to set up the nonprofit so that it operates distinctly from the church, it will still be in your best interest to maintain a positive relationship between the two organizations.

The church has the potential to add a great deal to the ministry of the nonprofit. As I have mentioned previously, the congregation can provide funding, volunteers, in-kind donations, and connection to community organizations and businesses. In addition, church members can be the best ambassadors for the nonprofit, spreading the message of your good work throughout the congregation and the community.

Also, there are risks to not cultivating the relationship between the church and the nonprofit. If you have tied the structure of the two organizations together in any way, the congregation may have the potential to stop new ministry dead in its tracks, if key staff and leaders of the church are not supportive of the nonprofit. This opposition could, for example, hinder the launch of new ministries, the release of the resources you need, or the purchase of property.

Even if you choose board model 3, in which the church and nonprofit remain completely separate in their structure and governance, avoid behaving as if the two organizations have kissed each other good-bye, never to speak again. When you envision the two separate circles in model 3, try to picture lines of communication running between the two. My experience has been that the strong support of your church congregation can only add to the success of the nonprofit. Use creative communication tools to garner that support.

Communicating with the Congregation

As mentioned numerous times throughout this book, the church congregation can be one of the nonprofit's greatest assets, and communicating with them can help release the time, talent, and treasure that the nonprofit needs. Think of church members as the first place to look for resources. Whatever they give can be used to leverage even more from businesses, foundations, and other external partners.

Here are some creative options for keeping communication going between the nonprofit and the church.

1. Use the church's own written communication vehicles to tell the story of the nonprofit. Use articles in the church bulletin and church newsletter to inform the congregation about upcoming events, recent successes, and stories of the people who are benefiting from the ministry. Do not just report what happened at the last board meeting, but use stories of transformed people to get church members excited. Also, try to include photos whenever possible.

    If the nonprofit sponsors a summer camping ministry for youth, for example, people in the church will love to hear the stories of individual youth and what they gained from their summer experiences. Have the kids write the articles and include plenty of photos of them canoeing, fishing, biking, and so forth.

    One caution: whenever you want to write a story about an individual participant, be sure to protect that person's right to remain anonymous and to keep the details of their situation confidential. This is especially important for ministries that reach out to extremely vulnerable people. For example, if a participant in your ministry is struggling with addiction or an abusive relationship, you should not give names or personal details when communicating about the program. In this instance, you could use statistics and general information about the entire group of participants to communicate about the program's success (for example, 60 percent of participants have been drug free for the past two months).

2. Make regular appeals for volunteers for the nonprofit's ministries. Church members who are tutoring a child each week, for example, will carry that story back into the congregation and get others excited about what you are doing. Successful volunteer placements bring more volunteers and more money from the congregation.

3. Share updates and testimonies from the pulpit. It may be difficult to squeeze some time for the nonprofit into an already "packed" Sunday morning worship service, but if you can do it, it will be well worth it. This is just about the only time when the congregation is your "captive audience." It is a great opportunity for you to tell a compelling story of the work of the nonprofit, perhaps through personal testimonials of volunteers or participants in your programs. It is also a great time to recruit volunteers or to highlight opportunities to make financial gifts to the nonprofit. You will probably need to keep it short (in most congregations three to five minutes would be appropriate)—if you want to be invited back to speak again.

4. Preach a sermon about the work of the nonprofit, or ask one of the pastors to do it. This is a surefire way to build inspiration and understanding within the church congregation. Some congregations let program staff preach periodically—perhaps the executive director of the nonprofit could be added to that schedule. Or if preaching is not that person's gift, one of the pastors could focus a sermon on a Scripture that is related to the work of the nonprofit.

   I served on a church staff that asked four program directors to preach "mini sermons" on the book of Nehemiah. We all preached for a couple of minutes each on one Sunday morning and the congregation loved it. Each of us gave our own perspective on how the story of Nehemiah was related to the urban ministry work of the church and the nonprofit in rebuilding the community.

5. Do your own mailings to church members. In addition to using church publications to get the word out, you will need your own brochures and newsletters devoted exclusively to the work of the nonprofit. Try to do your mailings at times of the year when the congregation is not inundated with other written information from the church (such as Easter or in the fall when church programs have their kick off).

6. Include stories about the work of the nonprofit at major church events. If the church has an annual dinner, see if you can secure some time for a slide presentation or short video about the nonprofit and the ministries under its umbrella. It is a great time to highlight what has happened during the past year and to look ahead to new programs, new opportunities for volunteer service, and new opportunities to give financially.

7. Sponsor special events just for church members. You may want to bring in a special speaker for a weekend of events, including a Sunday morning service. If part of the work of the nonprofit is to build affordable housing, for example, you could invite a nationally known speaker with a housing ministry to address the people of your church. This will help you educate the congregation about the issue and give you an opportunity to promote the work of the nonprofit.

8. Include information about the nonprofit as part of the new member process or new member class. If possible, send someone from the nonprofit to speak to the group. Also, include the nonprofit's brochure or newsletter in any written information given to new members. Some new members may be more attracted to the church because of its affiliation with a nonprofit that is doing valuable work in the community.

9. Speak to small groups or Sunday school classes about the nonprofit. While it may seem less efficient to address 10 people at a small group instead of 1,000 at the Sunday morning worship, I have found that intimate settings like these often draw in the most committed volunteers. You will have more time to tell the story of the nonprofit's ministry, and the people in the group will have more opportunities to ask questions. Come prepared to present some volunteer opportunities that entire groups like this could engage in. Increasingly small groups and covenant groups are including service to the community as part of their mission. For example, give them opportunities to paint a classroom, or prepare dinner for the welfare-to-work class.

10. Hold an annual recognition or thank-you dinner for program volunteers and financial supporters. These types of events are another great opportunity to tout the successes of the nonprofit and describe your needs for the upcoming year. Personal testimonials by volunteers or program participants (respecting confidentiality issues, as described previously) can be a great way to inspire the people in the audience to do even more in support of your ministry.

Negotiating Communication "Space" for the Nonprofit

Many churches run so many programs for their own members as well as the community, that getting some "space" to inform people about the work of the nonprofit may be challenging. How can you inform the congregation about the nonprofit, when the youth ministry, adult education, Sunday school, and trustees are all trying to do the same thing? (I've worked with some churches that had 20 or more ministries all vying for the congregation's attention.)

First, if the church already has an organized communications plan for how ministries publicize themselves, be sure to get the nonprofit on the list. Some churches have a calendar for who gets to speak from the pulpit, who gets bulletin inserts, and who is given space for newsletter articles. Include this as part of your annual planning process and sign up early.

Another strategy: Negotiate for a special focus on the nonprofit at certain key times of the year. If you know you will need a new influx of volunteers in January, for example, ask for pulpit time or for a special feature in the church newsletter. Or if your nonprofit offers events and seminars, focus your communication around the fundraising and registration for these events.

Also, instead of competing with the other ministries of the church, you may want to see how you can work together to get the word out to church members. Perhaps some ministries with related purposes could recruit volunteers jointly.

When I directed the Park Avenue Foundation, I found that three ministry areas, including the foundation, wanted to solicit contributions from congregation members at year-end. Instead of inundating the congregation with three separate requests, the foundation, Cornerstone (the food and clothing ministry of the church), and the World Missions Commission did a consolidated appeal for funds. This was less confusing for church members, and I believe it helped us raise more money because the congregation felt good about the variety of ministry initiatives that the church was sponsoring. We asked people to consider giving to all three ministry areas and many did just that.

Maintaining Positive Relationships with Key Church Staff

The Pastoral Staff

It is critical for the pastoral staff to be well informed about the nonprofit. Pastors should be aware of the various programs of the nonprofit and their successes and should also know about organizational issues or developing challenges. Information is key to gaining your pastor's support, and a pastor who supports the nonprofit is more likely to lend the support of the church to the nonprofit's work. This extends to large matters like financial support from the church, as well as to small ones like making an announcement from the pulpit or using the church bus. A pastor who has a negative feeling about the nonprofit may feel it should be "on its own" with regard to funding, volunteers, and facilities.

Regular communication with pastoral staff is also important so that the work of the nonprofit and church can be coordinated. If your church is large, someone besides the pastor, such as the church administrator or office manager, may be responsible for some of the following details. Depending on how your church operates, it may be important to coordinate the following:

- calendar for special events
- communication about the nonprofit to the congregation
- fundraising and volunteer recruitment from the church congregation
- recruitment of church members for board and committee positions
- involvement of church staff in nonprofit programs

Some church-based nonprofits formalize the senior pastor's relationship with the nonprofit by making her or him president of the organization or a member or officer of the board of directors (see chapter 8: Personnel Issues). This ensures that the senior pastor is at the table in a formal way for nonprofit business. It also helps keep the church and nonprofit missions aligned and eases communication with church staff and board members.

If your organization chooses not to have the senior pastor assume a formal role within the nonprofit, be sure your executive director or nonprofit board chair has the chance to communicate with the pastor on a regular basis. One church-based nonprofit leader I know has secured a commitment from the senior pastor to meet with him once each month. This may seem like a minimal commitment, but this is a large, evangelical "megachurch" with a senior pastor who is a popular author and speaker. Setting aside time each month was a major commitment for the pastor, and a strong expression of his support for the work of the nonprofit.

Other Key Staff Members

Church staff members can hinder or help the work of the nonprofit. If the staff sense that you value what they think and they are included in discussions about the nonprofit, they can bring a great deal to your new organization. I have seen church program staff share their program expertise, volunteers, community connections, and supplies and equipment with the nonprofit. I have also watched church staff who have been left out of the discussion undermine the nonprofit by influencing church leaders and pastors to see the new organization in a negative light. From my experience, you can largely determine which response you will receive from the church staff based on whether or not you keep key people on the staff informed and involved.

Get church program staff involved in the formation of the nonprofit—do not shut them out of the process. If you work in a church where everyone guards their program "turf," it may be a little scary to get the program staff involved in discussions about the nonprofit, but from my experience, it is the only way to get past the "turf stuff" and begin to work together. You might be surprised how willing people are to give their opinion and expertise if you just ask them. Depending on the type of ministry you will be pursuing under the nonprofit, key program staff people to involve might include: the children's pastor, youth pastor, adult education director, associate pastor, family ministries director, or community outreach pastor.

Start the process of working with church program staff by gathering their input before the nonprofit launch. One-on-one conversations or staff meeting discussions might do the trick. You may also want to include several church staff people on a steering committee that is developing a plan for the nonprofit.

After the new organization is formed, be intentional about keeping church program staff involved and informed. Seek their input as you develop new programs under the nonprofit. Have ongoing conversations about how the nonprofit can coordinate with church programs. Church program staff could serve as informal advisors to the nonprofit in their area of ministry. If the nonprofit wants to launch a youth mentoring program, for example, learn all you can from the youth pastor about young people in the area and what they need.

Positive relationships with the administrative staff of the church will also help the work of the nonprofit. Be intentional about treating church clerical, bookkeeping, and maintenance staff with respect. Most church offices operate within certain procedures and deadlines. If you will be working with the church office staff in any way, learn what the procedures are and abide by them. I have found that the golden rule is a good idea in all aspects of life, but it is especially true when working with church office staff. If you turn in your invoices on time and give plenty of notice when copying needs to be done, you will be more likely to get that last minute check for supplies just before you leave on the camping trip.

Relationships with Lay Leaders

It is not just the paid staff members at a church who can hinder or help the nonprofit. In many congregations, lay leaders also play a critical role in the development of any new initiatives.

Formal Lay Leaders

Recognize the important role of formal lay leaders such as church board members and committee chairs by communicating with them on a regular basis. Work hard to negotiate some time for a report on the nonprofit at each church board meeting. The executive director of the nonprofit should make the report, or if you do not have this position in your organization yet, the pastor could make the report. A key program director or nonprofit board member could report as well.

Even a three-minute update will keep key church leaders informed about what the nonprofit is doing. Be sure to tell the story of your successes—help the church board "see" what it is you are accomplishing. Financial information, including the current "bottom line" and any key grants and contributions that have been received, are also useful pieces of information for the church board members.

It is essential to keep the church board posted on major challenges you are facing, preferably as soon as possible after the issue arises. In my experience, church boards do not like to hear about problems for the first time when it is too late to do anything to respond to them. An example of an update on a challenge: you had planned to launch a new program this fall, but are having to postpone because local foundations have not been forthcoming with grants. Let the church board know as soon as possible after the grants requests are turned down, rather than waiting until the fall when board members might be wondering where that new program is.

Maintaining this communication with the church board on a regular basis will make it easier when the nonprofit needs the church's help to move ahead on something later; for example, launching a new ministry, buying a building, or changing its bylaws.

Having at least one board member who serves on both the church board and the nonprofit board is also a good idea. This gives the nonprofit a formal voice at church board meetings, and keeps nonprofit staff aware of questions that the church board may have about the nonprofit. This person would serve in addition to any church or nonprofit staff members who also serve on both boards. For example, you may decide that the senior pastor of the church and the executive director of the nonprofit should serve on both the church and nonprofit boards. Choosing a lay leader who serves on both boards as well (as described above) will aid the ability of the church and nonprofit to communicate with each other even more effectively.

If your formal lay leaders have retreats or planning sessions annually or more often, make sure the nonprofit is included on the agenda. This would be a good time to give an annual report on successes and challenges of the past year and to alert the church board to any upcoming changes or proposals.

Informal Lay Leaders

There are people in each church congregation who have no formal title or position, but who exercise considerable influence nonetheless. Sometimes they are long-time members of the congregation who are respected by all for their sacrifices and hard work over the years. Sometimes they are people who represent a constituency—the elderly members who dislike contemporary music, for example, or the people who want to see more women in leadership in the church. From my experience, informal lay leaders can be your greatest help or your most frustrating hindrance when trying to move a new idea forward in a church.

Avoid overlooking these informal lay leaders as you are planning for your nonprofit. At the very least, you will need to understand what their opinions are so that you can prepare responses to their objections or concerns. One option is to include informal lay leaders on the steering committee that develops a plan for the nonprofit. Another option is to have some one-on-one conversations with key people and prepare your materials so that their concerns are answered. If there is one church member who always wants to know "who is in charge" or "what is the bottom-line cost," come to meetings prepared to answer those questions.

Keep Your Congregation Engaged

Sometimes when a new nonprofit is formed, the nonprofit's leaders feel such a sense of relief about being separate from the church that they forget about all the wonderful things that the congregation can bring to the ministry of the nonprofit. Indeed, it can be a relief to be separated from church politics, difficult people in the congregation, and the "way we do things around here" that come with being a part of a church's program.

But engaging the congregation can only make the work of the nonprofit that much more effective and powerful. Always be searching for creative ways to inspire your church members to give generously of their time, money, and expertise. Think of the involvement of your congregation as a part of the recipe for the nonprofit's success. They can add an enthusiasm, a generosity, and an understanding of the heart of the ministry that may not come from anywhere else.

Key Questions

Maintaining a Positive Relationship with Your Church

What communication tools will you use to communicate with your congregation? (Check all that apply.)

____ church bulletin
____ church newsletter
____ announcements from pulpit
____ church special events
____ sermons
____ nonprofit's brochures or newsletters
____ new member classes or packets
____ presentations to classes or small groups
____ nonprofit special events
____ church board meetings or committee meetings

Communicating with Your Congregation

Establish a schedule for communicating with the congregation about the nonprofit. Identify each communication tool and when it will be used during the calendar year; for example, you might include a story about the nonprofit's work once each quarter in the church newsletter.

Who are the key church staff members you need to stay in close communication with? What strategies will you use to communicate with them?

Who are the key church lay leaders who you need to stay in close communication with? What strategies will you use to communicate with them?

Are there any informal leaders of the church who should be "in the loop" regarding the nonprofit? List them.

12

Evaluating Your Progress

Now that you have put all of this work into setting up your nonprofit, you need to realize that it is possible to change what has been put into place as necessary. You will need to "test drive" your nonprofit for a while (perhaps a year or more) to see what works and what needs improvement. Then once you have been operating for a period, you can pull together a group of people to evaluate the progress of the organization and to recommend changes.

The board structure that you chose just isn't working? Revisit it with your board and staff and change it so that it does. Does the mission still seem unclear? Then work to refine it. Most changes like this take a great deal of work, so I would not recommend that you pursue them lightly, but I think too many organizations act like they are "stuck" with the status quo, when a few alterations would make all the difference.

Regular evaluation of the nonprofit will help make the organization stronger and more effective. If you are committed to evaluation, I recommend that you set aside time each year specifically to review the successes and challenges facing your group. In my experience, it takes so much time and effort to actually run a nonprofit that it is difficult to make time on a weekly or monthly basis to evaluate what it is that you are doing. Pick a time once a year when the nonprofit's workload is not quite as heavy and schedule an all-day retreat, a series of meetings, or a special event that your stakeholders will participate in. Scheduling it far in advance will communicate that it is important and will give your stakeholders an opportunity to get it on their schedules.

One note: this chapter focuses on the evaluation of your entire organization rather than the evaluation of a single program. Program evaluation is also vitally important in the life of your nonprofit, because it helps you determine the impact of your efforts. In evaluating programs, you need to establish measurable outcomes and answer the question: "How have people's lives been changed as a result of participating in the program?" Consider using a program evaluation consultant to help you develop effective evaluation tools. There may also be an evaluation training program in your area that could help a staff or board member develop the skills your group needs to assess program effectiveness.

Working with Stakeholders

The point of evaluating your organization is to identify what needs to be changed in order to help your group better achieve its mission. Change within an organization will be longer lasting and less traumatic if key stakeholders are invited into the process of making the changes. Stakeholders can help you identify the issues within the nonprofit and develop a process for change. Depending on how your organization operates, some or all of the following stakeholders might be appropriate for you to involve.

1. Board of Directors. Your Board should be able to provide you with feedback on the big picture; for example, monitoring overall finances, seeing how programs fit into your nonprofit's mission, awareness of staff member's performance.
2. Staff. Staff input is also invaluable, as they can testify to what it is like to implement the decisions made by the organization. Avoid asking only your executive director for input; rather, be sure to include program staff and other key staff members including the office manager as well as support and building maintenance staff. The people in support positions are often the most keenly aware of glitches in the system.
3. Volunteers. In smaller organizations in particular, program volunteers can also provide great feedback on what it is like on the "front lines," carrying out the organization's mission. They can often tell you what works and what does not work in very specific terms.
4. Program Participants. Surveying program participants will help you gauge the impact of your programs and the public's perception of them. You may want to work with a program evaluation consultant to add questions to the survey below that will get at the measurable outcomes of the nonprofit's programs.

5. Congregation Members. Asking for the input of church members will give you a sense if you are communicating effectively with the congregation. Work to find out if members know about the activities of the nonprofit, and if they do, what are their impressions of the organization?

6. Community Members. The people in your neighborhood will be able to tell you what they know about the nonprofit and what it is like to interact with the organization. If yours is not a geographically based nonprofit, your community might be a demographic group; for example, pastors in your denomination or emerging women leaders.

Key Questions for an Evaluation Process

Listed below are some key questions to ask about your organization on a regular basis. There are several ways to present the questions to your stakeholders and to gather their feedback.

- A written survey is a good way to gather feedback and get people thinking before you have a meeting or event. Make sure to send it far enough in advance of your meeting (probably two weeks ahead of time) so that people have time to complete it and send it back.
- An all-day retreat for board and staff can help you surface key issues, talk them through, and develop a work plan for the coming year. Using an outside facilitator to lead such a session may be more effective than using a facilitator from inside your organization. Outside consultants can frequently see things that insiders cannot and may be less afraid to ask the tough questions.
- A series of meetings may work better for you if your stakeholders are unable to devote an entire day to a retreat. Also, if you have a number of difficult issues to work through it may make sense to break up the discussion a bit and give people time to think and process between sessions.
- A special event may work well if you decide to involve the community or a large group of volunteers in your process. Make it celebratory so that people will want to attend. You might want to break the large group into smaller focus groups to give more people the chance to express their opinions.

Mission and Vision

Does the nonprofit have a mission and vision that is understood by the people in it (staff, volunteers, and board members)? If not, what do you think needs to be done about it?

What progress have you seen the nonprofit make toward achieving its mission?

What else needs to be done?

What, if any, are the obstacles that stand in the way of the nonprofit making progress toward its mission? List them.

What ideas do you have about ways to overcome these obstacles?

Board Structure and Function

Is the current board structure of the nonprofit helping the organization achieve its mission?

If not, what changes to the structure would you recommend?

Does the board make decisions quickly enough? How do you think the decision-making process might be improved?

Are additional board members needed who will bring new skills and connections to the nonprofit? What new skills or connections do you think are needed?

How could the board structure be modified to enhance recruitment?

Fundraising

Has the nonprofit been able to raise the funds needed to support the programs that are its highest priority? If not, how much money is needed and for what?

Has the nonprofit met its fundraising goals for the past year? Has the nonprofit been able to secure enough funding to begin new initiatives?

What strategies would you recommend to secure additional funds?

Personnel

Has the nonprofit been able to recruit the number of staff it needs to run the organization's programs?

Has the nonprofit been able to attract staff with the qualifications and experience needed? If not, what steps should the nonprofit take to recruit the staff it needs?

Legal Issues

Has the nonprofit received its 501(c)(3) designation from the federal government? If not, what steps need to be taken to complete the process?

What other legal issues need to be addressed? Who should address them?

Communication

Does the nonprofit communicate adequately with the people in the congregation and the community? If not, what strategies would you recommend?

The following can be addressed to congregation members or people in the larger community.

Name two events sponsored by the nonprofit this year.

Name two programs that the nonprofit sponsors.

Name one volunteer opportunity available through the nonprofit.

A Work in Progress

My first years spent in the nonprofit sector were frustrating ones because I wanted to have a sense of being "done" with my work at some point. I did not like that things kept changing constantly—board members would come and go, funding would increase then decrease, new programs began, and others were completed. What I have learned through 15 years of work is that in any healthy organization there is constant change. The one thing we can control is how we respond to it.

So after you have gone through the challenging process of setting up a nonprofit at your church, do not be surprised if the need to change what you have established presents itself pretty quickly. Constant change does not indicate that you have made a mistake somewhere along the way—it is just a part of living in the nonprofit world these days. A commitment to regular evaluation of the organization will help you manage change and achieve your mission more effectively. I also think it can make involvement with the nonprofit more fun and less frustrating. Articulating your successes can be so uplifting, and putting your frustrations on the table can be a big relief. Working through both can draw the people in your group closer and lead your organization on to even greater success.

Appendix

Engaging Your Congregation in the Housing Crisis

by DeAnn Lancashire

No single entity can accomplish as much as groups working together. If government, churches, businesses, financial institutions, and educational institutions combine their commitment, strategies, and resources, communities in the United States will be able to rebuild poor neighborhoods, making them communities of hope and opportunity for social and economic justice. One housing advocate and activist has been quoted as saying, "There are more churches in America than there are homeless families." What would happen in our communities if every church adopted a homeless family—or made affordable housing a priority?

Churches and faith communities are in a unique and vital position to help solve the housing crisis, as well as other social ills. Biblical injunctions, in the Old and New Testaments, make very clear our obligation as people of God to help people in need.

> Is not this the fast that I choose? . . . Is it not to share your bread with the hungry, and to bring the homeless poor into your house; when you see the naked, to cover him; and not to hide yourself from your own flesh? (Isa. 58:6)

> If you see a brother or sister in need and do nothing to help them, how can the love of God be in you? (1 John 3:17)

As communities of faith, we are the body of Christ. We are God's hands: God's emissaries to the poor; we are God's voice: God's advocates for the poor. When we pray, "Thy kingdom come, thy will be done, on earth . . ." we are in effect agreeing to cooperate with God by bringing to our world God's design for communities of peace and justice.

The members of your church have a wealth of skills and knowledge as well as roots in the community. In your congregation there are teachers, city officials, social workers, business people, real estate brokers, contractors, bankers, and others who are aware of the many needs in your neighborhood. Some have immense financial resources. Some in your midst have very few tangible resources but can give firsthand accounts of their needs and struggles. As a gathering place for people of faith, no other organization is better equipped, spiritually and materially, to address the needs of the poor in your community. Together, with the proper understanding, guidance, and organization, the people of your church can work toward making God's kind of community a reality.

What Can Faith Communities Do?

Given our many gifts and resources for helping people in need, churches might use a wide variety of strategies to address housing-related needs in their community. One possibility is to create a 501(c)(3) nonprofit corporation. If your church decides to use this strategy to carry out a ministry dream, you will find invaluable the guidance provided throughout the book. Whether the need to be addressed by a nonprofit is the low reading levels of many children in the local elementary school, lack of safe places for youth to gather after school, domestic abuse, or lack of affordable housing, the process for developing the nonprofit remains the same.

Whether you are considering starting a nonprofit to address housing needs in your community or have in mind other approaches, the first and most important step is to educate yourself and your congregation about the housing crisis. This will take time, effort, and dedication, although you can begin with simple steps to help get you started and then take on more ambitious efforts after you begin to understand the issues in your area. Initially, you might use the following summary of the crisis to raise awareness in your congregation about housing issues. Housing issues differ greatly from one region to another, so you will also want to do further research about the housing needs in your state, county, and neighborhood, and also share that information with members of your church.

The Crisis

Homelessness and housing issues are complex. Factors determining the severity of the problem vary from region to region. One glaring problem, however, is found across the entire nation: a decreasing supply of affordable housing units. A 1998 study by the Center for Budget and Policy Priorities found major housing shortages in almost all of America's 45 largest metropolitan areas, as well as in rural communities.

Housing is considered affordable if 30 percent or less of family income is spent on housing costs. This means a family making $3,000 a month should spend no more than $900 a month on rent and utilities combined. According to National Housing Data, there are only 40 affordable units available for every 100 low-income renters. Right now, more than five million low-income American renters spend 50 to 80 percent of their income on housing costs, leaving very little for other necessities. For them, the threat of homelessness is real, especially if they should suffer a major illness or accident, or lose a job or a spouse.

The lack of affordable housing in America is causing severe social problems, including more homelessness among the working poor. The 2001 U.S. Conference of Mayors from 27 U.S. cities reported an average 22 percent increase in requests for emergency shelter assistance from homeless families alone. Fifty-two percent of these requests went unmet. And the problem is getting worse. All over America shelters are full; affordable housing units are full; waiting lists are full; and every day hundreds of thousands of people are turned away empty.

For every homeless person in a shelter or on the streets, many more live in unstable or temporary housing situations. Staying in cheap hotels is often the last step before becoming homeless. Evidence shows that many women, especially those with children, will stay with abusive partners rather than face homelessness. Others survive by doubling up with another family, which creates overcrowding problems.

Overcrowding, a common result of a lack of affordable housing, is defined as one or more persons per room, not including bathrooms and hallways. For example, four persons living in a one-bedroom unit with a kitchen, dining area, and living room is considered overcrowded. Studies show that children from at-risk or overcrowded home environments suffer chronic illnesses, learning difficulties, and behavior problems at a much higher rate than children in adequate housing. In addition, overcrowding is illegal and such families risk eviction and may end up on the streets.

Roots of the Affordability Problem

Social scientists, researchers, and analysts point to several issues as sources of the housing shortage.

The Affordability Gap

The increasing numbers of poor renters combined with the declining numbers of affordable units has created the worst affordability gap on record. Despite the apparent growing economy in the 1990s, work wages did not keep up with cost of living and rent increases. Between 1974 and 1993, rent climbed 13 percent and wages decreased by 8 percent.

Loss of Formerly Affordable Units

Public outcry against "slumlords" and drug houses has resulted in the demolition of much of what used to be affordable housing. Rundown firetraps and old public housing projects are being torn down and replaced by offices or market-rent units, too expensive for low or moderate-income families. Thousands of families are being displaced by demolition, and little is being done to help them. In the meantime, many cities have stopped accepting applications for assisted housing programs, because waiting lists are so long.

The Section 8 Wait

The Section 8 rent-subsidy program works on a voucher system and reimburses landlords a portion of the rent. People applying to the program have an average 20-month wait to become certifiably eligible for Section 8 housing. After certification they can apply for a Section 8 voucher, which they need to have in hand to show potential landlords, but the wait for vouchers takes up to 22 months. By the time they get a voucher, Section 8 renters have another wait: it takes an average of 16 months for a unit to become available. This translates to a nearly five-year wait. To further complicate matters, landlords are becoming more reluctant to let apartments to Section 8 participants, and in today's tight rental market they have little reason to do so—they can always find someone in a higher income bracket to rent the space.

Increasing Costs

Affordable housing can be an oxymoron. Land is expensive, not to mention the costs of contractors, materials, permits, and fees needed to build housing according to strict building codes. Although these higher standards in building codes ensure safer buildings and environments, they also ensure high rent and mortgages. Developers often need several funding sources for one affordable housing project. This means several different lawyers and accountants will need to be involved as well. The costs and complications entailed often delay and sometimes even kill the entire project.

Neighborhood Resistance

The American public does want something done about homelessness and the housing crisis—as long as it happens in someone else's neighborhood. Whenever affordable housing is proposed in a moderate-income neighborhood, a nonprofit developer often faces red tape and intense resistance. Many neighborhoods pass strict zoning regulations to exclude affordable housing. This "Not In My Back Yard" attitude, or "NIMBYism," has killed many nonprofit affordable housing projects.

NIMBYism is a product of people's stereotypes and fears of the unknown. Folks who protest against proposed housing projects often make erroneous speculations about what "might happen" if affordable housing goes up in the neighborhood. One man, whose father had Alzheimer's, obtained a special permit to remodel a large family home and provide care for up to 10 older people. Neighbors vehemently opposed this, making the usual complaint about lowered property values, erroneously adding that children might find used hypodermic needles in the yard (National Low Income Housing Coalition, NIMBY Report, January 2002). As ridiculous as these speculations can be, neighborhood resistance often grows out of such improbable, fear-inducing scenarios.

There are three main fears behind NIMBYism.

1. Fear: "Affordable housing lower property values." When people think of low-income housing, they think of ugly high-rises, cheap-looking buildings, and unkempt slums.

    Fact: Deteriorating housing lowers property values. Research shows that contemporary affordable housing does not contribute to lower property values. In fact, modern affordable housing is safe, can be very attractive, and can foster community spirit and neighborhood pride (Affordable Housing Design Advisor: www.designadvisor.org; Congregations in Community, St. Paul Area Council of Churches).

2. Fear: "Low-income housing leads to an increase in crime." People think that drugs, gangs, prostitution, and violence will inevitably follow a low-income development.

    Fact: Affordable housing developments have strict admission and eligibility standards. Residents are screened; various support services help residents grow and remain productive members of the community (HUD: www.hud.gov; Congregations in Community, St. Paul Area Council of Churches, 2001).

3. Fear: "Residents won't 'fit in' with the neighborhood." This fear is often disguised racism or class-ism, which are themselves based on fear.

    Fact: Most people needing affordable housing are already members of the community. When neighbors meet and get to know the affordable housing residents, their fears are usually dispelled. They may even volunteer to help promote the project (National Low Income Housing Coalition, 2001: www.nlihc.org; Congregations in Community, St. Paul Area Council of Churches, 2001).

Lack of Political Will

Government policies have turned away from housing assistance in recent years. Housing is such a complex and controversial issue that politicians rarely use it as a platform for rallying support. For the sake of balancing the budget, the government has made major funding cuts in the Department of Housing and Urban Development (HUD). Little money is available for subsidizing rents anymore, and the Section 8 housing program is being downsized—to the point of becoming nearly nonexistent. The resulting crisis of homelessness and lack of affordable housing has been called by some "the problem that cannot be solved."

In order to take on this problem, HUD has been proposing legislative changes for housing development, working to get housing for the chronically homeless, and taking steps to prevent at-risk people from declining into homelessness. But the government admits it cannot do it alone. According to Andrew Cuomo and Mel Martinez, former and current HUD secretaries respectively, faith-based organizations working in partnership with community groups are vital to the success of government housing initiatives. Therefore, HUD has created the Center for Faith-Based and Community Initiatives, which offers incentives, technical assistance, and guidance to churches and community groups working together to improve their neighborhoods.

Our Saviour's Lutheran Church Housing Program:
From Homelessness to Wholeness

Our Saviour's Lutheran Church (OSLC) in Minneapolis has acted on the biblical injunctions to care for those in need. Located in the Phillips neighborhood—notorious for drugs, crime, and intense poverty—this congregation has a heart for its community. Although members never intended to set up a homeless shelter or transitional housing, that is exactly what grew out of their simply responding to neighbors in need. At that time there were no blueprints available for helping the homeless. OSLC learned through trial and error.

1982—Church staff members were involved in several neighborhood groups, one of which helped Native Americans get good jobs. Despite their best efforts, a single component consistently prevented people from obtaining and sustaining work: lack of sufficient housing. Many employers will not consider a job applicant who has no permanent address; and without the security of a home, people simply cannot make the transition to secure employment. OSLC's outreach committee began to realize the enormity of the problem and began discussing ways to address it.

Every night hundreds slept in alleys, doorways, and window wells. Some died from cold and exposure. The city of Minneapolis sent out a plea for city congregations to help in this "short-term" crisis by opening their church basements to homeless people during the winter.

Our Saviour's Lutheran and two other churches led the way in responding. Eventually 13 inner-city Minneapolis churches opened their basements to the homeless. They provided a warm, safe shelter and some folding chairs. Volunteers from the congregation took turns staying the night with up to 40 people, mostly single men, who slept in OSLC's basement that winter.

1983—The next fall, OSLC opened its "warming center" again. The congregation's English as a Second Language (ESL) program for neighborhood immigrants met in the basement a few afternoons a week. These meetings ended just before the homeless came in for the night. The ESL folks always had food left over from their meetings, so they invited the homeless people to finish it off. Shelter volunteers saw how hungry the people were, and they brought this need to the congregation. More volunteers came to serve hot meals at night and provide food for breakfast.

1986—OSLC hired a director and staff for the shelter and recruited more volunteers from 10 to 12 other churches. In order to ease the burden on OSLC's outreach board, a separate shelter board was formed. The shelter now operated year-round, providing food, mats, bedding, and rudimentary laundry facilities for the bed linens.

Late 1980s—The plight of America's homeless population was now well known. Despite the efforts of government and churches, the problem persisted and even worsened. Conservative voices argued that homeless people *choose* homelessness. Many churches closed their basement shelters due to lack of volunteer support. Of the 13 churches in Minneapolis that operated shelters, OSLC was one of only three congregations that continued sheltering the homeless.

1991–1992—Instead of giving up, OSLC partnered with two other churches and bought two properties as transitional housing. They got MHFA loans, forgivable after 20 years if the facilities were used only for transitional housing. In 1991 they bought a six-bedroom duplex next door to the church, and in 1992 a former treatment facility on the next street, which provided 10 bedrooms after renovation. In these facilities, each person had his or her own bedroom: the women in the six-bedroom duplex and the men in the 10-bedroom building. With case management, including goal-setting and strict guidelines, people began moving into employment and permanent housing.

Many of those who had successfully transitioned came back to volunteer at the shelter and help others as they had been helped.

1994—OSLC's basement was the center for much of church life, as well as for outreach programs. The homeless shelter, the growing ESL program, an after-school program for kids, and various church committees all had to share the space. Among problems with timing and space was the issue of cleanliness. The basement was terribly smelly—a natural outcome of 40 unwashed people sleeping there every night. A medical clinic just four doors down from the church offered to sell their building to the shelter board. It could be renovated into an emergency shelter, and the homeless would not need to share the church basement. The offer seemed an answer to prayer, but there was no money for the venture.

1995—OSLC's much beloved senior pastor of many years resigned to take a position in the synod office. Church members were moving out of the rough neighborhood, and the congregation began declining in numbers. The night before the children's Christmas pageant, an enormous fire gutted the church. The people sleeping in the basement were saved and relocated to a space made available through Community Emergency Services. The shelter board was able to get a permit to operate a shelter there, but it was only temporary.

OSLC held their worship services in the chapel of the Lutheran Social Services headquarters building across the street. As the congregation grieved the loss of their pastor and their building, their numbers continued declining. What should they do? Build? Fold? Merge with another church? After much discussion and prayer, the congregation decided to make the housing program a priority. With the first insurance payment, they gave the shelter board the money to buy and renovate the medical building. The shelter board agreed to raise money to pay the church back. It took over $200,000 and armies of volunteers to get the place fixed up and running.

1998—Our Saviour's Housing began operating as an emergency 14-hour shelter, offering 40 beds, showers, laundry facilities, a gathering room/dining hall, and full service kitchen. Two full-time case managers set high expectations for the people in the program. A resident must get and keep a job, save money, and look for housing, as well as obey the shelter's strict rules banning drugs and alcohol.

This program has become the most respected in the Twin Cities' shelter-ring community.

2000—Our Saviour's Lutheran built a new church facility. In place of the towering stone fortress of 1912, a white street-level building with floor-to-ceiling windows faces a busy corner bus stop. Its openness welcomes the community. As a symbol of OSLC's inner-city nature, they incorporated concrete sidewalks as walkways through the foyer, into and around the hardwood floored sanctuary. The basement is now completely devoted to ESL and GED programs.

2002—In addition to the 40-bed emergency shelter, Our Saviour's Housing operates two transitional housing units for single men and women, and a large house used as transitional housing for three families, next door to the women's transitional duplex. It also has a cottage for the caseworkers' offices. Our Saviour's Housing is still a program of the church, but for liability reasons, it is in the process of becoming a separate 501(c)(3) nonprofit organization. The entire housing program operates on a $600,000 budget.

Our Saviour's Housing's 30 to 35 percent success rate for clients finding permanent housing would be higher if more affordable housing were available. Residents work hard to find work, save money, and deal with their personal issues, but often they are unable to secure a place to live before their time in the shelter expires. They are allowed a maximum of 90 days (including extensions) in one shelter, but that is often not enough time to overcome all their obstacles. Many residents must move on to another shelter or the street instead of into an affordable apartment.

Sandra Aslaksen, current director of Our Saviour's Housing, cites NIMBYism, low wages, and political apathy for the continuing lack of affordable housing. When comparing the number of available housing units to numbers of homeless, she says, "We're going backwards! There have never been more sheltered beds available—but though all the beds are filled, there have never been more homeless people on the streets."

Basic Education

In order to help members of your church understand the need to address housing issues in your community, you might want to begin with some of the following activities:

- Include information provided in the above summary of housing issues for newsletters, bulletin inserts, and education forums to provide an orientation to the issues.
- Visit various facilities in order to get different perspectives on homelessness and housing issues. Such facilities include emergency homeless shelters, transitional housing, and permanent affordable housing.
- Contact your local Housing and Urban Development office to learn about your community's homeless assistance plans. This plan lays out the need for assistance; what housing and services are being provided to meet those needs; the gaps between the two; and what the community is proposing to fill these gaps.
- Talk to homeless people. Befriend a homeless or low-income family struggling with housing issues. Find out what life is like for them.
- Find some local churches that are addressing housing or community development issues and invite speakers to your church.
- Volunteer at a homeless assistance facility or a building project, such as Habitat for Humanity.
- Learn about the various support services for the homeless and low-income renters. Services might include job training and placement, medical, chemical and mental health, ESL, GED preparation, literacy, child-care, teen programs, and legal assistance. Many organizations and facilities offer housing and services at the same location.
- The Internet is an excellent educational tool. You can learn a lot about housing issues, find organizations in your area, and discover a project you would like your church to become involved with or emulate without ever leaving your computer. Listed at the end of this appendix are Web sites and contact information of various organizations addressing housing, homelessness, and other related topics.
- Print out some of the fact sheets from the National Coalition for the Homeless and the latest issues of "NIMBY Report" from the National Low-Income Housing Coalition, and read them to your board or congregation.

Poverty Simulation

When your group is ready to learn more, you might want to take on more complex educational strategies. Many groups are doing poverty simulation exercises, a powerful educational experience. These "games" put participants into a variety of situations that low-income or homeless people have to face every day. Through role-playing, participants must navigate the welfare or shelter system, try to find housing, and encounter stereotyping, and many other demeaning, frustrating obstacles that keep them from achieving security and success in life. There are a variety of games for different ages. Most games take one to three hours, including debriefing and discussion. You may modify the curriculum and use it for weekly classes or do a one- or two-day poverty immersion experience.

Poverty simulation teaches through experience, not mere information. It captures the imagination and breaks down stereotypes; it creates awareness and empathy; it makes statistics real. Only by understanding the others' experiences can we know how to do unto them justly and mercifully.

Poverty simulations require one or more leaders or facilitators. Some churches prefer to have an outside organization facilitate their games. Local faith-based homeless shelters or housing advocates may conduct such simulations or may be able to refer you to an organization that does. For instance, Congregations in Community of the St. Paul Area Council of Churches facilitates simulations at Minnesota churches. Some homeless shelters hold on-site simulation games for volunteers and youth groups.

The Bay Area Homelessness Program (BAHP), a consortium of 16 California Bay Area colleges and universities, offers the Homeless Education Kit, a free resource for simulation games, through their Web site: www.thecity.sfsu.edu/~stewartd/welcome.html. These innovative games are designed to teach church groups, community groups, faculty, and students about issues related to poverty and homelessness. From the welcome screen click "Education." You can download the free materials from the Web site or e-mail BAHP (bahp@sfsu.edu) to order through regular mail.

Educating Children and Youth

Young people have an acute sense of justice. When they become aware of someone in need or encounter injustice, they immediately want to do something about it. Allow the young people in your church to learn and get involved. It is our obligation as adults of faith not to squelch their enthusiasm, but provide opportunities for children to be part of bringing about social justice.

Many children in suburban or middle-class areas, however, have no idea there are low-income children hurting just a few miles away. Many adults have a tendency to want to protect children from the harsh realities of life, but telling children about others in need is not going to harm them. It will only teach compassion and a desire to help. Allowing and facilitating children's participation in social justice is one of the Godliest things we can do for them, for we are empowering them to be sensitive, caring people with life patterns of creative activism. If we could harness their energy, kids could help change the world.

The Web site for the National Alliance to End Homelessness, listed in the resource section at the end of this appendix, has some excellent free educational materials available for downloading and printing. There are different age-appropriate materials for various grade levels, all of them engaging and inspiring. These could be used in Sunday school or mid-week classes along with biblical texts advocating mercy and justice for the poor. Such texts include: Isa. 58:1-12; Matt. 25:31-46; 1 John 3:17; Ps. 68:1-10, 84; and Luke 4:16-22.

Starting a Discussion Group or Think Tank

Another strategy is to find people in your congregation who are already involved in or know something about housing issues, such as developers, contractors, landlords, renters, architects, bankers, real estate brokers, social workers, and "neighborhood experts": people who work for the city, schoolteachers or administrators, and neighborhood business people. Create a vehicle for them to share their skills and experiences, and they may create a vehicle for creating change.

Julie Madden, coordinator for St. Joan of Arc Catholic Church's Peace and Justice Department in Minneapolis says she had no problem getting a committee of such people together. She called parishioners who had some kind of involvement or employment in housing, telling them the church wanted to get more proactive about the housing crisis. "We need your expertise and we want to create a platform for your stories," she said. Every person she called accepted the commitment gladly. According to Madden, people will jump at the chance to be part of something that is close to their hearts, especially when they can use their gifts and experience to help others.

St. Joan of Arc Catholic Church:
A Housing Summit

St. Joan of Arc Catholic Church formed a leadership council made up of 12 people who were housing, financial, and neighborhood experts. They held a "Housing Summit" once a week for 10 weeks. In order to define their mission they asked: "In an ideal situation, how would a faith community address the housing crisis in *our* area?" If every church asked itself this same question there would be many different answers. St. Joan answered it by creating a collaborative ministry of four teams:

1. The Dream Team—architects, contractors, and others with housing development experience—identifies potential neighboring properties for rehab or development.

2. The Shared-Space Team works with homeowners who are willing to share their living space with others.

3. The Adopt a Family Team—working with school officials and social services—identifies a homeless or at-risk family. During the two-year transition from homelessness to secure housing, the family receives transitional housing, and emotional and financial support.

4. The Leadership Support and Service Team facilitates the other teams and works to ensure their success.

The 10-week Housing Summit culminated in a Housing Sunday—a theme carried from pulpit to religion classes. Children drew pictures of houses, which lined the walls of the gym, and wrote letters to their mayors asking what they were doing about housing issues. Many kids received personal responses and thanks from their mayors.

The Housing Summit was an eye-opener, even to a church like St. Joan that was already involved in affordable housing. For years, St. Joan had been renting out a house to a low-income family at below market rate. They operated two hospice homes for adults living with HIV/AIDS and were heavily involved in affordable housing advocacy. Before the summit, many people in the congregation, and even some on the council, assumed there was nothing more they could do to make a difference in their community's development, because the neighborhood appeared to be already built up and developed. On closer inspection, the Dream Team found 20 to 30 properties nearby that were condemned, empty, or with liens on them. These have been marked for possible future development.

At the time of this publication, St. Joan is still in the process of growing its housing program. They hope to partner with other faith communities to create a strong network of housing provision and advocacy. Although their story is still unfolding, St. Joan's process offers an excellent model for others to follow.

Next Steps

At this point your church should have a fairly good idea of your community's particular housing issues. Perhaps, as happened at St. Joan's, your discussion group will evolve into a committee or team. At some point you will most likely need to form one or more teams or committees.

The following questions, similar to ones used by Congregations in Community of St. Paul, are designed to elicit discussion and help your group determine its focus and mission.

1. Why are you interested in creating housing or home ownership opportunities for people of color and the poor?
2. In your opinion, why is the creation of affordable housing for low-income and people of color often fought against?
3. How should the community hold organizations, agencies, and governmental bodies accountable for creating affordable housing?
4. What entities in the community should lead the campaign for creating housing and home ownership opportunities for low-income people?
5. What affordable housing strategies do you think hold the most hope for success?
6. How should faith communities deal with public policy regarding housing and home ownership opportunities for the poor and people of color?
7. How can we work together and partner with other groups to strengthen our efforts? With whom should we partner?
8. How can we make sure that low-income people are ensured a permanent place in the planning and decision-making processes on issues that affect them?
9. What is in it for us as an organization to be proponents of affordable housing?
10. What do you as an individual need to get out of the effort?

People who work in successful housing and service programs highly recommend intentional relationship building and collaboration with other groups. In Richmond, Virginia, Strategies to Elevate People (STEP) social services programs emphasize the importance of proceeding "carefully, cautiously and with commitment; avoiding fads, abstaining from quick fixes, and building quality relationships with community and people of good will."

There is no set formula to tell you how to progress. Every church and every area's needs are unique, and there is plenty of room for innovation as well as replication in creating affordable housing. Your church must pray and work together to figure things out; however, if you follow the suggestions of educating yourself and your congregation, if you form discussion groups and committees of informed people, if you walk by faith and not by sight, a way will open.

Advocacy

Another step members of your faith community might take is to become advocates for affordable housing. Charitable projects and advocacy often go hand in hand, and experts in affordable housing say it takes a combination of charity and advocacy to get things done. However, not everyone is cut out for advocacy. Some people will gravitate more toward research, planning, and development; others will be more inclined to work quietly behind the scenes to provide practical help. But those with activist tendencies can be encouraged to put their energies into advocating for affordable housing.

Of course a church does not need to have a 501(c)(3) to do advocacy or provide special services, but as your congregation begins planning and developing its nonprofit, certain public policies and attitudes in your community, such as zoning laws and NIMBYism, will need to be faced. Local officials and politicians are affected by the same attitudes, myths, and fears as those of their constituents. They will need to be educated, appealed to, and maybe even pushed before your nonprofit is free to do its work. Advocacy and lobbying require education and experience in order to be effective—and legal. Groups listed in the resource section at the end of this appendix provide information and guidance as well as links to other activist organizations.

Starting a Nonprofit at Your Church

Careful research and planning are essential if your congregation is thinking about addressing housing-related issues. In particular, keep in mind that even the experts disagree about whether it is necessary or appropriate to establish a nonprofit corporation to carry out the particular ministry to which a congregation feels called. Our Saviour's Lutheran Church, whose history was reviewed above, worked with housing issues for years before setting up a corporation. But Sondra Ford, director of real estate development of the Faith Center for Community Development (FCCD) in New York City, emphasizes the importance of starting a separate 501(c)(3), especially before any programs or real estate developments take place. She cites three main reasons for setting up a nonprofit:

1. A nonprofit corporation helps your church protect its assets. Your church runs the risk of being held liable if someone becomes injured on the premises or as a result of your group's activities. Keeping the nonprofit and church separate is a much safer course to take.
2. Grant makers such as government agencies and foundations are more likely to contribute money to a corporation instead of a religious group. They usually prefer to fund faith-based corporations that provide community services to people no matter what their religion.
3. A faith-based nonprofit can be a wonderful way to bring many different kinds of people together. Your church's nonprofit could include on the board people from other neighborhood religious and community groups—a great testimony to the world of unity and love in action.

Starting a nonprofit takes a great deal of planning, many resources, and much commitment, and it should not be undertaken lightly. Churches and other faith communities will want to work carefully through the chapters of this book to define the ministry dream and take the steps necessary to establish this type of nonprofit. Organizations listed at the end of this appendix are available to help churches with this intimidating, but not impossible, process.

Community Development Corporations

Churches and other religious communities all over America are tackling various problems in their own neighborhoods by creating specialized nonprofits called community development corporations (CDCs). In addition to affordable housing projects, CDCs may address health care, day care, after-school activities, substance abuse counseling, job training, ESL classes, life skills education, home-ownership promotion, and small business loan programs. As your church becomes more in touch with the housing crisis, you may feel called to provide such specific support services in addition to affordable housing or to supplement an existing housing program.

The needs are many and varied. Some churches focus on housing for seniors or the developmentally or physically disabled. Other faith communities feel called to provide housing and care for teen mothers or single parents, people living with HIV/AIDS, or women and children suffering from domestic abuse. People who struggle with substance abuse, runaway youth, and migrant farm workers are others who might have special needs. Some support programs and services provide practical help and education; others enable people to build their own capacity for success. Truly revolutionary in scope and mission, community-building projects that address such needs are improving the quality of life in low- and moderate-income communities.

Lawndale Christian Development Corporation:
A Housing Rehabilitation Initiative

Lawndale Christian Development Corporation (LCDC) in Chicago (winner of a FMF Maxwell Award) is a great example of neighborhood housing rehabilitation. While the Department of Building was busy demolishing deteriorating apartment buildings, LCDC got busy renewing them—creating safe, affordable housing.

LCDC partnered with Local Initiatives Support Corporation, worked with a community bank to get a first mortgage, and obtained a second no-interest, 40-year payment-deferred mortgage from the city. They qualified for an energy grant and renovated two abandoned apartment buildings, now known as Tabernacle Apartments. Tabernacle Apartments has 26 units and accepts Section 8 vouchers. Residents pay no more than 30 percent of their income for rent. The clientele includes families, seniors, those with physical disabilities, single parents, and single adults. LCDC also has a day care center, and offers health and social services through its health center and church.

To read more about Lawndale Christian Develop-ment Center and other fine projects, go to www.fanniemaefoundation.org and click on Maxwell Awards of Excellence.

Overcoming Barriers

Faith-based groups encounter all kinds of obstacles to their projects, whether organized as a legal nonprofit corporation or carried out in some other manner. In addition to the usual difficulties that come when working with people, you will face institutional fortresses, which are not built to suffer change. The education and partnership organizations listed in the resource section can help you prepare for and navigate around such barriers as obtaining startup, program, and staffing funds; staffing gaps; federal, state, and local regulations; discrimination, and many other unforeseen difficulties. The more complex your initiative, the more thought you will want to give to resources and strategies for overcoming barriers. A number of possibilities are available.

1. Working with government agencies. Some states, cities, or counties have a state faith-based and community initiatives liaison or someone in a local office or agency whose role it is to connect faith-based organizations to the appropriate government agencies. It is a good idea to work with one of these officials early in your development process.
2. Tailoring the program. Another important strategy for overcoming common barriers is to tailor your program to the needs of the people in your area. If you do your homework and get to know the people in need of services, you will be more likely to create a successful program. An excellent way to do this is to conduct a "listening campaign." Talk to low-income people in your church or community: visit churches in poor neighborhoods and ask the people about their housing concerns, the problems they face, and services they lack. Include at least one or two low-income people or people of color on your committee or teams; it is only just and right that they take part in developing the programs that will have an impact on them.
3. Drawing on member's skills. It is also vital to grow your program according to the skills and experience of your parishioners. People have a hard time getting excited and involved in programs they have not helped develop. They may feel as if they are being made to fit into prefabricated "boxes" or roles and will not be able to sustain interest and enthusiasm for long. On the other hand, people who are invested in a project will commit themselves to it. A program with enthusiastic, committed volunteers will attract other volunteers with like passion.

The most successful programs are ones that address the needs of the community while building upon the expertise, stories, and energies of the people of the church.

4. Establishing partnerships. Building steady partnerships with churches and other organizations will also help reduce the turnover rate and strengthen your nonprofit. Find a few people with good networking, communication, or fundraising skills who will commit to building partnerships. Let them work to create a campaign of mutual investment, so other churches, community groups, and local businesses can feel some ownership in your organization and its efforts. Educate those partnering congregations using the principles and suggestions discussed earlier, such as poverty simulation.

   One inner-city transitional housing program provided a way for nearby suburban churches to take ownership in its projects. The volunteer coordinator enlisted three different churches to help buy three different buildings. Each church raised money and awareness, sending volunteers to help rehabilitate and furnish its unit. A healthy competition and unifying camaraderie developed among the various volunteers; this in turn created a connection of community between the urban and suburban neighborhoods. Each facility was named after each church, and those churches now feel the responsibility and desire to maintain an active presence in their projects. They built unity along with transitional housing units—a unity that continues to enrich their lives and neighborhoods.

5. Working with businesses. Consider working with your local banks and other businesses as well as other churches. One Minnesota bank gives substantial annual contributions to Our Saviour's Housing and also sends meals and volunteers every month. Complex projects depend on the stability that partnerships provide.

6. Learning from success. Studying other successful faith-based housing and service projects will help strengthen the development of your own nonprofit. The Fannie Mae Foundation's Web site publishes profiles of their Sustained Excellence and Maxwell Awards recipients. These stories prove that with determination and the right connections, faith-based nonprofits can overcome incredible obstacles and create wonderful opportunities for justice and renewal in even the most desperate neighborhoods.

Your church can play an important role in helping to change society by actively addressing housing issues in your neighborhood. It will be an exciting adventure, but it will not be easy. Like all pioneers, you will face frustrations, barriers, and even dangers to your mission. There may be times when you feel like giving up, but if you organize, pool your many resources, and work together, you will discover a new way of life; a way of life that vitalizes your church and community. Individually and corporately, the people of your church will learn valuable lessons. Your faith will be challenged in many ways, but it will become stronger as it becomes more practical and tangible.

Strategies to Elevate People: A Partnership Effort

In Montgomery, Alabama, two black and five white congregations came together to address their town's problems of poverty and homelessness. The stability those seven churches created became a foundation for building an inTer-racial consortium of 26 churches representing 10 denominations. The congregations' leadership knew it would take working with other groups to make their project successful. They partnered with financial institutions, federal agencies, and private businesses and raised $270,000 of in-kind donations.

Over 500 volunteers provide a variety of social, spiritual, and supportive services to residents of nine public housing developments through a program called Strategies to Elevate People (STEP). These strategies work to end homelessness, and develop self-sufficiency and economic opportunities for Montgomery's poor. The STEP program has benefited not only public housing residents with an elevated sense of pride in self and community, but the city at large, with lower incidence of crime and greater trust between races. Housing authorities in Alabama have studied this highly successful program in order to imitate it elsewhere. Montgomery's STEP program continues to grow.

The Montgomery story won HUD's former Best Practices and Profiles, an initiative that unfortunately has been suspended due to budget cuts.

Resources

General Background

Building Prosperity and Abundance in Your Community: A Guide to Launching a Financial Education Program in Your Church. Published by the Faith Center for Community Development, Inc., and the Fannie Mae Foundation. For ordering information, call (212) 785-2782.

Putting Faith in Neighborhoods: Making Cities Work through Grassroots Citizenship by Stephen Goldsmith. The story of how Indianapolis invented a national model for creating vibrant urban centers through encouraging citizenship and engaging faith-based organizations. Published by the Hudson Institute. Order through the Hudson online bookstore: www.hudson.org.

Rebuilding Our Communities: How Churches Can Provide, Support, and Finance Quality Housing for Low-Income Families. A 280-page resource manual published by World Vision. Cost: $15.50. All prices include postage and handling. Send order request and check or money order to: World Vision, Mail Stop 310 P.O. Box 9716, Federal Way, WA 98063-9716.

Housing Issues, Homelessness, and Advocacy

Building Healthier Communities (www.mcauley.org)
BHC is a wonderful resource for faith-based groups interested in community development. Click on "Healthy Community Resources" for an exhaustive list of links to other organizations.

McAuley Institute
8300 Colesville Road, Suite 310
Silver Spring, MD 20910
Phone: (301) 588-8110
Fax: (301) 588-8154

Charity Lobbying in the Public Interest (www.indepsec.org)
From the Independent Sector homepage, click on "Charity Lobbying in the Public Interest." Educates nonprofits about the importance of lobbying and

advocacy, and how to do it appropriately, effectively, and legally to achieve your organization's mission.

The National Alliance to End Homelessness
(www.endhomelessness.org)
Check out the "Best Practices and Profiles" of organizations doing great work. Click on "Fact Sheets for Kids" to download and print age-appropriate information, worksheets, and projects for grades K–12, which make excellent faith and justice education materials.

> 1518 K Street NW, Suite 206
> Washington, DC 20005
> Phone: (202) 638-1526.
> E-mail: naeh@naeh.org

National Coalition for the Homeless (www.nationalhomeless.org)
This organization works for justice in housing, economic opportunity, health care, and civil rights. NCH offers education, partnerships, and technical assistance for grassroots organizations and is active in political advocacy. This Web site is a wealth of information. Click on "Facts about homelessness" for fact sheets on various aspects of homelessness. Click on "Directories" and select your state from the pull-down screen to find links and contact information for an advocacy group in your area.

> 1012 Fourteenth Street NW, #600
> Washington, DC 20005-3471
> Phone: (202) 737-6444
> Fax: (202) 737-6445

National Low Income Housing Coalition (www.nlihc.org)
An excellent resource for education and advocacy. Check out the NIMBY report online. Click on the Out of Reach publication to learn more about America's growing wage-rent disparity and the extent of the affordability problem in your own community.

> 1012 Fourteenth Street NW, Suite 610
> Washington, D.C. 20005
> Phone: (202) 662.1530
> Fax: (202) 393-1973
> E-mail: info@nlihc.org

National Faith-Based Programs

Habitat for Humanity International (www.habitat.org)
HHI is a nonprofit, nondenominational Christian housing organization working to eliminate poverty housing. They welcome people of all faiths to help people in need build simple, decent, affordable houses. Click on "Find Your Local Habitat Affiliate" to contact a group near you.

Mercy Housing System (www.mercyhousing.org)
Develops, operates, and finances affordable and attractive service enriched housing; builds strong, healthy communities, and revitalizes distressed neighborhoods.

> 601 E Eighteenth Avenue, Suite 150
> Denver, CO 80203

National Interfaith Hospitality Network (www.nihn.org)
This nonprofit organization helps faith-based and community groups organize network programs that provide shelter, meals, and assistance for homeless persons. It also works to increase community involvement in direct service and advocacy.

> 71 Summit Avenue
> Summit, NJ 07901
> Phone: (908) 273-1100
> Fax: (908) 273-0030
> E-mail: info@nihn.org

The above listing is just one way to get you started. Most of these Web sites have links to other sites and organizations, but you can do your own Web search, too. Different search engines will yield different results, as will using different keywords. Try search engines such as Yahoo, All the Web, or Lycos using keywords such as:

"housing" + "crisis" + the name of your state or city
"affordable" + "housing" + "faith"
"church" + "affordable housing" + your city or state
"NIMBY"; "housing advocacy"; and so forth

Education and Partnership Organizations

Affordable Housing Design Advisor (www.designadvisor.org)
"A tool, resource, idea bank, and step-by step guide to design in affordable housing." This Web site is for those working to be part of the solution to the affordable housing crisis. The Affordable Housing Design Advisor is loaded with advice from experienced designers, developers, and builders from all over the United States. It is designed to help you at every step of the process of creating affordable housing. The gallery has beautiful photos and stories of successful, safe, and attractive affordable housing projects that incorporate the principles of "good design."

The Congress of National Black Churches (www.cnbc.org)
An excellent community and economic development program. CNBC partners with HUD and Fannie Mae to offer training and technical assistance to churches and other faith-based organizations seeking to bring economic opportunities to African Americans.

> 2000 L Street NW, Suite 225
> Washington, DC 20036-4962

Christian Community Development Association (www.ccda.org)
Compelling and challenging ideas for Christians wanting to live out their faith in service to the poor. Makes a plea for wholism: evangelism *and* social action.

> 3827 West Ogden Avenue
> Chicago, IL 60623
> Phone: (312) 762-0994

The Department of Housing and Urban Development (www.hud.gov)
This government site provides information and education about every aspect of home buying, renovation, and community development. Offers grants and loans, and helps interested organizations develop partnerships. See their Best Practices and Profiles for stories of churches and community organizations doing wonderful work.

Faith and Community at Work (www.faithandcommunityatwork.com)
This is an informational resource for faith-based organizations working for community economic development (CED). It helps faith-based groups understand what skills, resources, and planning are needed to carry out a CED project and provides access to technical assistance and training tools. This organization is a collaboration of the Federal Reserve Bank of Boston, the Fannie Mae Foundation, and the National Congress for Community and Economic Development (NCCED).

The Faith Center for Community Development (www.fccd.org)
This organization helps churches and other faith-based organizations organize, plan, and develop their own nonprofit community development projects. FCCD also offers organizational development grants and credit counseling, and teaches organizations where and how to access monies for further community development.

Faith in Communities (www.hudsonfaithincommunities.org)
A Hudson Institute initiative and active "Charitable Choice" supporter, this organization provides information, resources, and education to faith-based groups working on community development.

> 757 King Street
> Charlottesville, VA 22903
> Phone: (434) 293-5656

The Fannie Mae Foundation (www.fanniemaefoundation.org)
Dedicated to creating affordable homeownership and housing opportunities, FMF offers a wealth of education and partnerships to individuals and organizations in order to build healthy communities across the United States. Every year FMF offers grants, fellowships, and awards to various organizations, including churches, for developing housing programs. Visit their Web site to learn more about this invaluable resource.

National Center for Neighborhood Enterprise (www.ncne.com)
This organization provides training and technical assistance to faith-based organizations seeking to address housing issues, homelessness, deteriorating neighborhoods, as well as many other needs of the poor. NCNE also links organizations to other sources of support.

Bibliography

This bibliography is not intended to be an exhaustive list of resources on the topics I have covered in this book. Instead, I have chosen a few books and Web sites that I believe are particularly relevant to the work of setting up a church-based nonprofit. Some of the resources, though not all, are specific to faith-based organizations.

Barry, Bryan W. *Strategic Planning Workbook for Nonprofit Organizations, Revised and Updated.* St. Paul: Amherst H. Wilder Foundation, 1997.
    This book provides a five-step process to completing a strategic plan for your nonprofit, covering preparation steps, a situation analysis, and the writing and implementation of the actual plan. The book is easy to follow and covers just about any question that will arise during your planning process. I like the fact that this book does not offer just one "cookie-cutter" planning approach that will supposedly fit all nonprofits. You are given options, for example, as to how much time your organization would want to spend on strategic planning (in my experience, a critical decision that too few groups discuss), the number of people you would want to involve, and the length and scope of the final product.
    The worksheets included at the end of the book are helpful and will enable just about any group to complete the process outlined in the text of the book. The appendices include steps for planning with multiple organizations and a sample strategic plan from a community development organization.

Bernstein, Leyna. *Creating Your Employee Handbook: A Do-It-Yourself Kit for Nonprofits.* San Francisco: Jossey-Bass Publishers, 2000.

Creating personnel policies for a start-up nonprofit can seem like an overwhelming task, but this book will provide you with the information and sample policies you need for just about any topic area you choose to include in your employee handbook. This book is very comprehensive, covering a wide array of topics including hiring, termination, employee benefits, paid and unpaid leave, and harassment. The breadth of topics covered in the book may seem overwhelming, but if you work with your attorney or human resources professional to identify the key policies for your organization, the book can provide language and resources that will be a great help to you.

My favorite aspect of this book is that it identifies that small, medium, and large organizations will have different needs when it comes to personnel policies. So the author offers three different approaches under each topic area: the Creative Approach (for groups with up to 20 employees), the By-the-Book Approach (20 to 100 employees), and the Leading-Edge Approach (over 100 employees). If your nonprofit is small, for example, the author recommends that you keep your employee handbook simple, reflecting the less formal nature of your group.

A computer disk that contains all of the sample policies in the book is included.

Berry, Erwin. *The Alban Personnel Handbook for Congregations.* Bethesda, Md.: The Alban Institute, 1999.

Edwin Berry shares his many years in personnel management in a book that is chock-full of useful examples and specific policies and procedures. Berry takes into account the many unique aspects of hiring and managing personnel in a faith-based institution, including the role of the pastor and strategies for working with the church personnel committee and communicating with the congregation. A case study of "Stone Church" that is woven throughout the book drives home the author's points. The author also weaves values consistent with congregational life into his recommended personnel philosophy, emphasizing building trust, and treating employees with dignity, fairness, and concern. The appendix of the book is filled with sample forms and policies, including an employment application, a sample job description, an employee handbook, and a performance evaluation and improvement plan.

Because the position descriptions in the book focus on traditional church staff positions such as pastor and music director, you will need to seek out other resources to help develop positions for your nonprofit. For example, you may need additional information on adding the following positions to the nonprofit staff: executive director, resource development director, and specialist positions in program areas such as housing and economic development.

Carlson, Mim. *Winning Grants Step by Step: Support Centers of America's Complete Workbook for Planning, Developing, and Writing Successful Proposals.* San Francisco: Jossey-Bass Publishers, 1995.

This is a great resource on the actual writing of a grant proposal. The author emphasizes the need to fully develop program ideas before seeking funding for them—something that many nonprofits forget to do in the rush to get the money. The first sections of the workbook take the reader through a process of evaluating a new program idea—whether it fits with the organization's mission and strengths and whether it meets a real community need. There is also great information here on developing goals and objectives, evaluation measures, and an accurate budget. I like the worksheets in each chapter because they help the reader take concrete steps toward developing the proposal itself. The "Defining Clear Goals and Objectives" chapter, for example, includes a worksheet that asks the reader to identify each objective, its target population, time frame, and the change that will occur.

Carver, John. *Boards That Make a Difference: A New Design for Leadership in Nonprofit and Public Organizations.* San Francisco: Jossey-Bass Publishers, 1997.

This book is a summary of a popular board model developed by John Carver. The "Policy Governance" model is embraced by many people in the nonprofit sector, though certainly not by everyone. The author recommends that boards focus on big-picture policies only, rather than on management duties that should be delegated to staff. He also recommends that boards focus on "ends" rather than "means," expending time and energy on ensuring that the organization is actually making a difference and achieving its mission, instead of focusing on processes alone.

If you choose to have a navigational board for your nonprofit, that is, one that focuses on the big picture, this book will provide invaluable advice on how to implement that approach. I will say that the book is rather conceptual in its presentation, lacking the step-by-step information included in most other publications listed here. But if you invest the time to wade through this material, you will certainly glean a greater understanding of how boards can function.

One of the shortcomings of this book is that it does not define an explicit role for board members in fundraising. While it can be difficult to get board members interested in resource development, they can play an important and direct role in securing resources for the organization. Also, start-up nonprofits, particularly those run by very part-time staff or volunteers, may have a hard time applying this model, at least at the outset. There simply may not be enough time for paid staff to fulfill all of the management roles and duties of the organization, and board members may need to step outside of the policy realm as a result.

Drucker, Peter. *The Drucker Foundation Self-Assessment Tool: Participant Workbook*, rev. ed. Gary J. Stern. *The Drucker Foundation Self-Assessment Tool: Process Guide, rev. ed.* New York: The Drucker Foundation and San Francisco: Jossey-Bass Publishers, 1999.

Peter Drucker has developed an easy-to-use assessment tool that will help you answer five key questions about your nonprofit, once it has been operating for a period of time: "What is our mission?" "Who is our customer?" "What does the customer value?" "What are our results?" and "What is our plan?" The participant workbook and process guide provide step-by-step instructions on finding the answers to these questions. The process outlined here engages board members, staff, and key volunteers as well as primary and secondary customers of the nonprofit.

I like the fact that the Self-Assessment Tool "cuts to the chase"—the five key questions truly are the heart of the matter for any nonprofit. There are no tricky methods or group processes here, simply a focus on what the organization is trying to accomplish and where it should best focus its energies next. The Participant Guide is filled with worksheets that will be easy for anyone to use. There are also clear instructions on how to gather information from customers; for example, templates of surveys and interviews.

I have only two suggestions for using this material. First, this tool has not been designed with faith-based organizations specifically in mind. You may want to add questions about the "spiritual performance" of your organization, if that is critical to the achievement of your nonprofit's mission. Second, while the self-assessment process is easy to follow, it may seem overwhelming to you if your group is still relatively small. You may decide to streamline the materials somewhat as a result.

Dudley, Carl S. *Basic Steps toward Community Ministry*. Reprint, Bethesda, Md.: The Alban Institute, 1997.

This book provides invaluable advice for congregations that are deciding which community ministries to pursue. Making these decisions can be confusing without guiding principles or a practical process. Dudley provides both, using specific examples from nearly 40 congregations around the United States. The first section provides tools to understand the community around your church, focusing on listening to the people and identifying natural gathering places and structures in the community. Section 2 encourages congregations to let Scripture, their own history, and their strengths or limitations guide them in choosing ministry focus. The last section provides tips and advice on implementation, but start-up ministries will need more than what is included in this final section to put the proper systems for implementation into place.

Golden, Susan L. *Successful Grantsmanship: A Guerrilla Guide to Raising Money*. San Francisco: Jossey-Bass Publishers, 1997.

This book takes the reader through the entire process of submitting a grant proposal: researching possible funding sources, making first contact with the funder, preparing a proposal, and then following up. If grant writing is brand new to you, the chapters on preparing to submit a grant will be particularly valuable. Too many grant writing resources emphasize only what to write in the proposal itself. In contrast, this author devotes most of her chapters to helping the reader understand the funding dynamic—how to find funders, how to treat them when you meet them, and how to consider the whole grant making process from the funder's perspective. In my experience, those critical preparation steps can make the difference between proposals that get funded and those that do not.

There is also excellent information here on preparing a budget and following up with the funder once you have submitted a proposal. Winning Grants Step by Step (also listed in this bibliography) is a better resource for the writing of the proposal itself.

Harper, Nile. *Urban Churches, Vital Signs*. Grand Rapids: Wm. B. Eerdmans Publishing, 1999.

This book describes the journey of 28 urban churches toward revitalizing their congregations and reaching out into the community. Each church is featured in a separate chapter, with a "what we can learn" segment at the end of each. Many of the churches profiled in the book chose to set up a separate nonprofit (or several) to launch their new community ministry ideas. If your church-based nonprofit will be focused on community ministry, you might like to read these interesting stories, just to get a sense of what's possible through a separate 501(c)(3) connected to your congregation. The stories do not provide much "how-to" advice on setting up a nonprofit, but they do include quite a bit of information on why the various churches chose this path. A variety of denominations and ministry programs are featured in the book.

Hummel, Joan. *Starting and Running a Nonprofit Organization*, 2d ed. Minneapolis: University of Minnesota Press, 1996. Revised by the Center for Nonprofit Management, Graduate School of Business, University of Saint Thomas, St. Paul.

Though this book is not specifically for ministry groups, it does contain a great deal of helpful information for start-up nonprofits. The author writes in a style that is easy to understand—a great help to readers who have no previous experience with managing a nonprofit. The legal chapter stands out in particular, providing a concise, step-by-step overview of the process. I also like the chapter on writing the bylaws, which takes the reader through an extensive list of questions, with the answers providing much of the wording of the actual document. The section on developing a budget will also be very useful to a new nonprofit, providing an easy-to-follow template for identifying both expenses and income for a new organization.

Klein, Kim. *Ask and You Shall Receive: A Fundraising Training Program for Religious Organizations and Projects, Participant Manual and Leader Manual*. San Francisco: Jossey-Bass Publishers, 2000.

Kim Klein is a guru of grassroots fundraising, and over the years, she has helped many types of nonprofits, including small social justice organizations, find creative ways to secure the funding they need. This book (a participant manual and leader manual are available) translates her fundraising approach into a training program specifically for faith-based groups. As near as I can tell, her approach and content have not been changed in this new book, but she has inserted many examples and case studies that are specific to faith-based groups, particularly those focused on social justice, feminist ministries, and interfaith exchange. So depending on your denominational background and theology, you may or may not find ministry examples in this book that resonate with you.

I like the empowering approach that Klein uses in teaching fundraising; as you read her materials you will truly get the idea that anyone can raise money. The books are structured as a training series to be taught to a group. Topics covered include: the case statement, the role of volunteers, direct mail, special events, major gifts, and soliciting over the phone. Each topic is explained in easy-to-understand terms, and there are planning charts included in each chapter, providing a way for groups to start listing action steps in each area.

Kretzmann, John P., and John L. McKnight. *Building Communities from the Inside Out: A Path toward Finding and Mobilizing a Community's Assets.* Chicago: ACTA Publications, 1993.

This is *the* manual for asset-based community development, and it will be an invaluable resource for you if your aim is to start a nonprofit with a community development focus. McKnight and Kretzmann contend that too often, a "needs-driven" approach is used to design community-based programs. These authors argue that starting with a community's assets is a superior method, emphasizing what the people, associations, and institutions in your community have in their favor as they prepare to address challenges. The book looks at specific groups of people (for example, artists, youth, and elders) as well as types of organizations (hospitals, law enforcement, parks, etc.) and the assets they offer the community. I like the fact that the book does not just describe the most obvious groups to tap into, but it also highlights people and organizations that might otherwise be looked at as a liability or at the very least, remain unrecognized in the good they do for the community. Welfare recipients, for example, are listed as a group that can contribute to positive community change.

Pay particular attention to the chapter on the potential contributions of religious institutions to community development work. The chart in this section shows the many, many assets that churches bring to the table. Also, many creative examples of church-based community development are cited in this section. These examples might give you some ideas for how your congregation can go to work.

Mancuso, Anthony. *How to Form a Nonprofit Corporation*, national ed. Berkeley, Calif.: Nolo Press, 2000.

This book explains the legal process of forming a tax-exempt nonprofit corporation in easy-to-understand and interesting language—a rare thing indeed when it comes to this topic. The book is quite large, so you will probably not be able to (or want to) read it cover to cover, but I found that it is a great resource for understanding the legal definition of a tax-exempt nonprofit, steps to forming a nonprofit, and sticky legal issues that you may want to be aware of, including unrelated business income tax (UBIT). The book takes you through IRS forms step by step and also provides templates for bylaws and articles of incorporation. I flip through this book whenever I have a specific legal question, and I am usually able to find the information I am looking for rather quickly.

Because this book was not written for use by nonprofits in a specific state, you will need to gather additional information on what your particular state requires of nonprofit organizations. Another disclaimer: Nolo Press promotes "self-help law"; that is, they encourage people to avoid hiring a lawyer and to do it all themselves when it comes to legal matters. I do not agree with this approach and strongly encourage you to hire an attorney to help you form your nonprofit (see chapter 9: Legal Issues, in this book). Use this book to help you prepare for sessions with your attorney. The more knowledge you have of the legal process at the outset, the less time your attorney will need to take to explain it all to you (thus lower legal fees).

Queen, Edward L., II, ed. *Serving Those in Need: A Handbook for Managing Faith-Based Human Services Organizations*. San Francisco: Jossey-Bass Publishers, 2000.

The editor has pulled together some of the finest experts in nonprofit management and community development to address the management issues facing faith-based human services organizations. The book encourages a step-by-step approach, covering preparation, then capacity building, then moving beyond the provision of basic needs. The three chapters on fundraising provide the most practical advice in the book, and great "hands-on" information is provided in the chapters on financial accountability and controls and board leadership as well.

This book sets itself apart from a typical nonprofit management manual by offering materials that are tailored specifically to the needs and assets of faith-based groups. Some of the authors have woven in biblical references and specific examples involving congregations, though overall, the book includes few case studies. The final chapters of the book focus on specific types of ministries: economic development, health care, and youth services.

Web Sites

www.boardsource.org

This is the Web site of BoardSource, formerly the National Center for Nonprofit Boards. Follow the "Board Q & As" and "Frequently Asked Questions" prompts and you will find a comprehensive list of questions about boards and answers that will get you moving on the right track. Questions on the Web site focus on such issues as: the role of the board and its officers, developing a conflict of interest policy, planning a board retreat, and what to put in the board manual.

BoardSource also publishes a number of easy-to-follow written publications about boards, which can be purchased at this Web site.

www.mcf.org

The Minnesota Council on Foundations Web site includes a brief paper entitled "Writing a Successful Grant Proposal" by Barbara Davis that can be downloaded at no cost. Davis is one of the best-known grant writers and teachers in Minnesota—and for good reason. Her paper provides easy-to-follow steps to writing a grant, including pitfalls to avoid and answers to frequently asked questions. There is also a great worksheet here on developing a budget.

Once you get to the site, follow the prompts for "Grantseeking Resources."

Other Resources Used in Writing This Book

I used the following accounts of efforts by two congregations to establish nonprofits as sources for this book.

Barry, Patrick. *Rebuilding the Walls: A Nuts and Bolts Guide to the Community Development Methods of Bethel New Life, Inc. in Chicago.* Chicago: Bethel New Life, Inc., 1989.

Sanders, Cheryl J. *How Firm a Foundation: Eighty Years of History, Third Street Church of God, Washington, D.C.* Washington, D.C.: Third Street Church of God, 1990.